Praise for *Breaking Through Gridlock*

"A field manual for change agents on how to build bridges across differences and move from talk to action."

—Adam Grant, Professor of Management, The Wharton School, and *New York Times* bestselling author of *Originals* and *Give and Take*

"This book is not for the fainthearted, but if you truly want to change the world, it's essential. It challenges us—as advocates, as citizens, as humans—to identify our own motivations and assumptions to create common ground with those we oppose or avoid. It asks us to abandon certainty and righteousness to allow for new and different paths toward our goals. And it gives us the tools and the inspiration to do so."

—Gwen Ruta, Senior Vice President, Climate and Energy, Environmental Defense Fund

"Our country's future depends on our ability to reach beyond our echo chambers. Jay and Grant guide us through starting the conversations so crucial to our democracy."

—Van Jones, cofounder and President, The Dream Corps; CNN contributor; and author

"We need the creativity that can be harnessed from competing perspectives to craft a thriving organization and a thriving society. This book gives people the tools to take that on."

—John Mackey, CEO, Whole Foods Market

"Jason Jay and Gabriel Grant single out authenticity as the key to breaking through the conversational gridlock that afflicts so many of our public and private interactions. They highlight the traps we fall into, as well as promising pathways for working our way out of them. It won't be easy, but you can use the exercises they offer to practice sidestepping the polarizing moves we make without even being aware of what we are doing."

—Lawrence Susskind, founder of the Consensus Building Institute; Ford Professor of Urban and Environmental Planning, MIT; and Vice Chair, Program on Negotiation, Harvard Law School

"Whether you're hoping to shift your company, your community, or even yourself, Jay and Grant have produced an accessible and practical guide that will make you chuckle with recognition—then motivate you to get to work."

—Christine Bader, author of *The Evolution of a Corporate Idealist*

BREAKING
THROUGH
GRIDLOCK

THE
POWER OF CONVERSATION
IN A POLARIZED WORLD

Jason Jay
Gabriel Grant

BK·
Berrett–Koehler Publishers, Inc.
a BK Life book

Berrett-Koehler Publishers, Inc.
1333 Broadway, Suite 1000, Oakland, CA 94612-1921
Tel: (510) 817-2277   Fax: (510) 817-2278   www.bkconnection.com

Ordering Information

Quantity sales. Special discounts are available on quantity purchases by corporations, associations, and others. For details, contact the "Special Sales Department" at the Berrett-Koehler address above.

Individual sales. Berrett-Koehler publications are available through most bookstores. They can also be ordered directly from Berrett-Koehler:
Tel: (800) 929-2929; Fax: (802) 864-7626; www.bkconnection.com

Orders for college textbook/course adoption use. Please contact Berrett-Koehler: Tel: (800) 929-2929; Fax: (802) 864-7626.

Orders by U.S. trade bookstores and wholesalers. Please contact Ingram Publisher Services, Tel: (800) 509-4887; Fax: (800) 838-1149; E-mail: customer .service@ingrampublisherservices.com; or visit www.ingrampublisherservices.com /Ordering for details about electronic ordering.

Berrett-Koehler and the BK logo are registered trademarks of Berrett-Koehler Publishers, Inc.

Printed in the United States of America

Berrett-Koehler books are printed on long-lasting acid-free paper. When it is available, we choose paper that has been manufactured by environmentally responsible processes. These may include using trees grown in sustainable forests, incorporating recycled paper, minimizing chlorine in bleaching, or recycling the energy produced at the paper mill.

Cataloging-in-Publication Data is available at the Library of Congress.
ISBN: 978-1-62656-895-2

FIRST EDITION
22 21 20 19 18 17   10 9 8 7 6 5 4 3 2 1

Book design and composition: Beverly Butterfield, Girl of the West Productions
Cover design: Wes Youssi
Cartoon art: John Cox
Copyediting and proofreading: PeopleSpeak

To our children,
Vikram, Uma, Ariana, and Madeleine

Struggling with others is the definition of war
Struggling with oneself is the definition of peace
HAZRAT INAYAT KHAN

Contents

Exercises

Figures

Tables

Foreword

Some might say that the time for talking is over—that we have moved to such a polarized state that nothing much can be accomplished by conversation. It is now a win-lose world and we just need to be sure that our side, whichever that may be, wins. This is tantamount to saying that we are at war and it is down to battle tactics.

But whom are we at war with? The deep challenges in our world—climate change, destruction of species, profound inequity, underemployed and restless young people around the world, social instability, economies that produce a surplus of wealth and a deficit of meaningful work—were not produced by "the other." They were produced by ourselves. We have a way of living that simply fails to generate basic conditions for well-being for ourselves and for many other living systems with whom we share a small planet. In this war with ourselves, winners and losers have little meaning, and we are left chasing our proverbial tails. We unwittingly substitute frenzy, anger, and fear for any sort of genuine progress that benefits all.

My conviction is that a growing number of people understand this. They know the world must change. They know you cannot keep growing materially on a finite planet and that the mindless pursuit of material growth for its own sake today mostly drives increasingly unhealthy competition for "my share" of the material pie, whether among people or countries. They know, at some level, that it is not about "us versus them." It is about a new "we" in the sense of "What sort of future do all of us want to create?" Ironically, this understanding can make matters worse by widening the gap between what we see as needed and what we see as happening all around us.

Facing this reality, we all have basically the same choice: keep "fighting the good fight"—pursuing our favored definition of progress in a battle for control—or change. But what does this sort of change mean, and why is it not the same as "giving up"? First, it is not about working less in support of what you believe in. It is about working differently. Simply put, it is about realizing that there are outer obstacles and inner obstacles to real change. And, to effectively engage the outer obstacles without engaging the inner ones offers only an illusion of progress, just as does facing only the inner ones. The essence of the choice is doing both or doing neither. The real work is that of the reflective practitioner, cultivating effective action *and* enhanced awareness, addressing the problems "out there" while simultaneously discovering the impediments "in here."

So, in the end, as activists working to shape a better world for our children and theirs—as we are doing every day in every exchange when we are purposeful about our lives—it comes down to how we will approach the next conversation. Just as the great physicist Werner Heisenberg said, "Science is rooted in conversations," so is the same true regarding social change. Is our intent to win or to learn? Do we leave the conversation more connected with one another and more inspired about what is possible, or less so? Do we operate in service of a future that might emerge or of a past that binds us to habitual ways of thinking and acting?

Facing these transcendent questions, Jason Jay and Gabriel Grant offer a wonderful blend of guidance and practical help. They know that deep change is never only a matter of intention. It also always comes down to practice—having ways to approach day-to-day matters that continually open up our own awareness. They also know that this is never a solo journey but one that must be traveled with partners, people working together to continually discover what it takes to open head and heart in confronting today's profound change challenges.

As neuroscientists say, "Under stress, the brain down-shifts" and we revert to our most primitive and habitual patterns of behavior. This is no less true collectively. We can all see this downshift unfolding around the world today. If there is to be any real progress in addressing the profound issues we face, rehabilitating our capacities to listen to one another and genuinely talk and think together will be crucial.

Peter M. Senge
MIT Sloan School of Management
December 26, 2016

Preface
How this book came to be

Think about the last time you tried to have a serious conversation with someone who didn't already agree with you. How well did it go?

What if you could step into situations where political, social, and environmental issues have gotten people stuck? What if, in difficult conversations, you could stay true to yourself while strengthening your relationships and creating powerful new ideas and results?

Laura, a college senior, heads to the seaside for a last hurrah with her friends. Together, they'll bring a beautiful close to their four years of school and celebrate their upcoming graduation. On day three at the beach, one of her friends says he doesn't believe the science on global warming. She gasps in disbelief and berates him. The next three days are awkward for everyone. Later, stepping back, she realizes that her approach harmed the relationship and didn't convince anyone to think differently. She apologizes to her friend, but she also shares a fuller range of her thoughts and feelings about climate change. The new conversation restores their relationship and creates an opening for her friend to reconsider the issue.

Kevin, a young business development manager, is working for a fast-growing renewable energy technology company. He encounters a new idea that inspires him—and could transform the whole industry. Full of passion and energy, he runs straight to the office of the new CEO, a former venture capitalist brought in by new owners of the company. Kevin gives what he thinks is the most compelling pitch of his life. Gradually he sees in the cold expression on the CEO's face that something is terribly amiss. He flails for a minute, recognizes he's no longer welcome, and quietly backs away. He feels rejected and begins to consider whether this is an appropriate company for him anymore. After a period of reflection, he realizes that he didn't take the time to make his idea relevant to the CEO's own concerns or his language of financial return. His revised pitch works. The company launches a new service model that rapidly accelerates renewable energy adoption across the world.

Passionate about healthy living, Michaela repeatedly cajoles her mother to address her obesity. Every time, the conversation escalates into nagging, fights, and disappointment. Michaela realizes that her own antagonistic stance may be contributing to the problem. She shifts gears and acknowledges that she has been more interested in being right than in being helpful. She takes her mother to the grocery store and they plan meals together.

They enjoy three dinners together in the same week after not eating together for more than a year.

Stories like these aren't the norm. All too often, our well-meaning attempts to drive our agendas forward can get stuck in the noisy traffic jam of competing ideas, priorities, and ideologies. It is rare that we break through gridlock and produce the results we really want for ourselves, our relationships, and our world—but sometimes we do. We love these stories about the power of conversation to make a better world. We wrote this book because we want more of them, and we have ways to help.

Our journey

This book began as a collection of our own stories, reflection, learning, and experimentation. Both of us have taken on crusades for a better world, in roles as student activists, organizational consultants, and university teachers. Along the way we missed opportunities for productive engagement, and we created collateral damage with our families and colleagues. Sometimes we resolved that damage, but other times we just got stuck, amplifying the polarization around political, social, and environmental issues.

As time has gone on, we have learned together how to turn around these situations into important successes and we've been invited to help others do the same. Jason has worked with senior leaders in a wide variety of companies like Biogen, Bose, and Lockheed Martin to help overcome internal barriers and advance their sustainability strategies. At a top-tier business school, MIT Sloan, he elevated the Sustainability Initiative from a small, passionate group of students and faculty to a strategic cornerstone for the school. He has inspired hundreds of students at MIT Sloan to care about sustainability and make it part of their careers. Gabriel has built coalitions to protect the environment in conservative institutions and has developed communities of change leaders within and beyond the American heartland through the creation of Byron Fellowship. He has led trainings for corporate leaders in partnership with organizations like PwC, Starbucks, Whole Foods, New Belgium, Sustainable Brands, Retail Industry Leaders of America, and GreenBiz.

In the beginning, we publicly reflected on our own experiences—where we succeeded and where we fell flat. People asked us for "the curriculum," so we made one. We began running workshops about having authentic conversations when people don't agree and going beyond "preaching to the choir" on issues of sustainability and social justice. We developed the methodology within our own teaching, and we made the work available to others. This curriculum has been incorporated into courses at a number of universities, such as Cornell and the University of Michigan, by colleagues who demonstrated that our success was teachable and replicable. And we've been invited to work inside organizations and to provide training for sustainability professionals including vice presidents or directors from more than 150 major brands. Together, we've coached about two thousand sustainability champions.

Our workshop participants range from young activists to seasoned leaders, from undergraduates to corporate executives. Through the experiences they generously share, we gain a unique window into the pitfalls of advocacy. We also learn their stories of success, how people find pathways through gridlock and polarization toward understanding, agreement, and creative action. While our work started with a focus on environmental advocacy, it has grown to support a range of broader "progressive" movements for sustainability, social justice, and public health.

If there is one fundamental insight in our work, it is that there is no script, no set of talking points that will move our agendas forward. Getting a "stuck conversation" unstuck is not about finding "the right thing to say" but about making a more fundamental shift—a shift in who we are being. Polarization and gridlock persist when people clutch onto fixed perspectives, fixed ways of thinking and being in the world. People break through when they free themselves up and expand their thought and action repertoire. They get in touch with the future they really want to create, and they create a stance and way of being that is aligned with that future. From there, the words and conversations flow naturally. Through this process, we can navigate artfully in unexplored territory. We can respond authentically to people's resistance. We can be consistent with our values while exploring new ideas that emerge out of the tension with others' values. When we fumble, we can re-engage and keep the conversation going forward.

This is not a book about gridlock in the way we typically talk about it, as an abstract phenomenon somewhere out there in the world. Yes, it is relevant to our political gridlock and polarization, where dialogue rarely occurs among people with different ideologies and party affiliations. Yes, it is relevant to organizational or bureaucratic gridlock, where people with different priorities and agendas struggle to find alignment and take action. In all these cases, breaking through gridlock begins in a conversation. And we've discovered your best training can be in your most intimate moments of getting stuck—at the dinner table or a holiday gathering.

A note on our language

In some cases, "they" is intentionally used as a singular pronoun to promote the use of inclusive language.

Introduction
How to use this book

This is a book for you and for your work in the world. It is a field guide and workbook, with a series of exercises that thread through the chapters. It asks you to do some hard work that requires reflection and vulnerability. If you stick with it, your work with the book will help you communicate powerfully with anyone about what's most important to you. It will help you harness the power of conversation to transform polarization and gridlock into creative outcomes and stronger relationships.

In the chapters that follow, we will challenge your notions of advocacy, leadership, and authenticity. We will invite you to examine your own conversations, your own moments of getting stuck, and the common pitfalls we all encounter. We will create opportunities for you to change the conversations that matter to you. We will then help you advance this new approach to conversations in your organizations and as part of crafting larger movements.

If we all do this, we will be able to solve big problems, to create a better future together. Along the way, we can create a better world right now—strengthening our immediate relationships within our families, communities, and organizations while reaffirming our own sense of purpose and accomplishment.

Serious play

To join us on this journey, we invite you into a very particular spirit, that of serious play. If those words sound contradictory, they are meant to.

The "serious" part involves the focus required to reflect in detail on our experience. It includes the courage to face the moments when we have contributed to our own failure.

"Play" recognizes a few things. The first is that if we take ourselves too seriously, our reflection will stray into judgment or possibly despair: not only are society and the planet coming to an end, but it's all our fault! Looking at our foibles and our humanity with lighthearted compassion makes it much easier to sustain our focus and courage. In fact, the moment we can poke fun at ourselves is when we know we have learned something.

The second aspect of play is that it's something we do *together*. The complicated situations we face are not unique. None of the pitfalls we stumble into have been made exclusively for us. Part of the value of our workshops and this book is to recognize that we are not alone.

This book will be more useful, and more fun, if you draw others in to give you a hand. Neither of us recalls making a personal transformation without help, without working with someone who helped us challenge ourselves. At the end of chapter 2, we will ask you to find a buddy who can accompany you on the journey, so you can start thinking now about who that might be.

To get started with the work, we would simply like you to identify where in your life this book might help you explore and experiment.

Exercise 1
Where do you want to break through gridlock?

Find a piece of paper or perhaps a notebook you want to use over the course of the book. Take a moment to make three lists.

Make the lists in sequence, but leave some space between them because you may find that you identify issues for list 1 after you make lists 2 and 3.

List 1: What issues are you passionate about?

The issues you are passionate about could involve big geopolitical challenges, simpler issues like turning off the lights, and anything in between. You can list issues where you are highly engaged through your work, social media, and social circles or those where you are more quietly but seriously concerned.

To help you brainstorm, you might consider the following questions: What feels threatened that you would like to protect? What values do you find yourself standing for? What vision do you hold for your household, organization, community, nation, or world?

List 2: Which of your conversations end up polarized or stuck?

With whom have you found yourself advocating, arguing, or debating the issues above?

Who is on "your side" and who is on "the other side" of the polarization?

When and where does this debate happen (e.g., the dinner table, Facebook, the office, or the school lunchroom)?

Continued on next page

List 3: What conversations are you avoiding because you know they will get stuck?
Whom do you believe "just won't understand" your perspective about the issues above?

With whom do you believe it is just too risky to talk about these issues and your ideas? You might perceive that risk as ranging from mild discomfort to serious retaliation.

A note on the exercises

When you see an exercise presented in the text like the one we just shared, it is because we think this is the appropriate moment to do it. Our best advice is to pause your reading and get it done. Throughout the book we have laid out a sequence of exercises in which the output of each builds toward the next. We have drawn most of them directly from our workshops, where they have been refined over time to optimize their results out in the world. Others are designed specifically for the book, and we've worked with test users to refine their delivery and their results.

The reason for these exercises is that we are action biased. Put simply, you can't learn to harness the power of conversation without being in conversation. We know people who have read the book and skipped the exercises, and it has contributed to their thinking. If you take on the exercises, however, you are more likely to produce real results in your life than be left with thoughts about how you might produce results. You'll complete the process with skills you can use going forward and potentially teach to others who share your goals.

Through participating in the exercises, you will be able to create results that speak for themselves. One of our classroom participants took on the reflective work with a partner in class. She then built the courage and a new approach to change the conversation and shared the following in a reflection paper:

> I've been a vegetarian for decades now, sometimes off and on—but often religiously. . . . It's easy to make such a life choice for yourself when you are living alone. But last year I moved back in with my mother to lessen the financial burden of getting an MBA. My family is Persian—which makes being a vegetarian very difficult. Our diet is made up of chicken or beef kabobs and stews filled with lamb.
>
> I never set out to turn my family into vegetarians when I moved here. I simply tried to convince them of the importance of purchasing sustainable and humanely grown meats and animal products. But even this request had no effect. During our class exercise I realized it was because I would lace my request with emotional outbursts and accusations.
>
> The day after our workshop, my aunt made eggs for breakfast and tried to serve me some. I was about to burst into a lecture of the torturous existence of caged chickens. Instead I politely declined the eggs. My aunt asked why (she knows I love soft-boiled eggs).
>
> Earlier that morning we had bonded on our discomfort of having been in China. My aunt used to travel there for work regularly—and would always come back a little depressed from her trips. . . . We talked about how, despite the importance of buying friends and family

small gifts from travels, neither of us felt comfortable buying cheap knick-knacks for fear of how they had been made in order to be sold so cheaply.

I hadn't planned on having "the talk" that soon—but all of a sudden I realized the connection I could make. With my mother listening in, I explained to my aunt that the same thing that made her feel uncomfortable buying bargains in China was why I feel uncomfortable buying bargain foods. For the first time ever I saw a spark of understanding in her eyes.

As a family, we began a conversation not about why I make the choices I make, but why we make the choices we make. And at the end of it all, my aunt asked me how she can tell what kind of meat to buy.

The next day I came home to find a carton of cage-free eggs and organic milk in the refrigerator. My mom had gone shopping. It was mind-blowing.

introduction summary

- This is a field guide and workbook that includes a sequence of proven exercises to help you along the way.

- If you stick with it, your work with the book will help you communicate powerfully with anyone about issues that are important to you.

- We invite you to join in a spirit of *serious play*: having the courage to face moments when we have contributed to our own failure and to poke fun at ourselves and have fun in the process.

- *Do the work*: Ask yourself, Where do you want to break through?
    - What issues are you passionate about?
    - Which of your conversations end up polarized or stuck?
    - What conversations are you avoiding because you know they will get stuck?

1

How We Get Stuck

Breakdowns in conversation

When we wake up in the morning and catch the news, it is clear that big challenges are facing our world, now and in the future. We hear about people in faraway countries and in the neighborhood next door who are having trouble making ends meet. We hear about both obesity and hunger. There are droughts and floods, fires and storms. We hear about corporations creating jobs and the next miraculous innovation—and about the next environmental catastrophe, social exploitation, and the co-opting of our democracy. Then we spill our coffee (or our children do that for us) and we have to change our shirt and rush to work—off to live our lives.

We have a lot to consider regarding the future of our children, our children's children, and people around the globe. The issues seem tangled together. People might describe them using words like "social justice," "public safety," "sustainability," or "public health," but these words can feel hopelessly abstract. If we get a moment to step back and ponder these issues, we ask some fundamental questions. What are the most pressing challenges? How did they come to be? What should we do?

One of the biggest problems, we find, is that we have a *profound lack of consensus* about the nature of the problems or what to do about them.

We think differently about which problems are most important to address. We have different views about the ability of markets and governments to help. We have different relationships to science, scripture, and other ways of seeking truth. We often don't even agree on what is going on now, much less what we want or how to get there from here. We see gridlock and polarization in the news—and all too often in our communities and organizations as well.

So what can we do—how can we break through and create agreement?

Perhaps we need grassroots consensus building. But we worry: "Is there time for that?" The issues are pressing.

Perhaps we should target key decision makers, people in positions of power who can make a difference now.

Perhaps we should rally people who think like us, getting them to advocate: to vote, donate, boycott, buy responsibly, petition, talk to their organizational or political representation.

Each formula for action has one thing in common: having conversations with people.

The power of conversation

Cesar Chavez was a migrant farmworker who became one of America's great civil rights activists. A student once asked him how he organized. Cesar replied, "First, I talk to one person. Then I talk to another person." "No,

how do you *organize*?" the student insisted. Cesar re-
peated, "First I talk to one person. Then I talk to another
person."[1]

Through personally connecting with the people in our
lives, we can mobilize others to join our cause. They are
in our family, in our neighborhood, in our organization,
and in our marketplace. Some of the conversations we
have are with people who share our passions and views,
and we want to mobilize them into action. Some are with
people who are indifferent, and we want to inspire them
to care. Some are with people "across the aisle" whom
we want to debate and persuade to change. Harnessing
the power of conversation means taking each of these
opportunities seriously.

We occasionally encounter skeptics of this approach:
"How can we tackle big systemic issues like inequality
or climate change through one-on-one conversations?"
"Maybe if you are a CEO of a major corporation, then
your conversations have power, but mine don't." If these
thoughts are crossing your mind, consider a conversation between Melissa Gildersleeve and her mom, Joyce
LaValle, who was a regional sales manager for Interface
flooring.

Joyce remembers what happened one day when
Melissa, an undergraduate at Warren Wilson College,
was visiting home:

> I came home from the grocery store and they had just
> introduced plastic carrying bags. I said to Melissa, "Isn't
> this fabulous? I can put them all on my arm, carry sev-
> eral at a time. This is such an innovation." She just really
> lost it. She said, "That's really great, except you certainly

aren't thinking about the future or my future when you are celebrating that." It was kind of a rude awakening. I didn't get it . . . plastic bags . . . what were they made of, they would never go away. You couldn't throw them in the trash to break down. A whole conversation began then with Melissa.

When she read Paul Hawken's book *The Ecology of Commerce*,[2] she said, "You read it and then you know what, Mommy? I am looking at landfills and going to them . . . you should start understanding about carpet and how huge it is in the landfill. And it is not going to break down." That was another kind of a big awakening. That was the connective tissue to the job I did and the harm that was being caused as a by-product. She sent me the book. She said, "Read it, and understand it, and make sure Interface understands it. Because something has to change." She knew I worked at Interface and thought I could do something about it, or at least bring it up.

Joyce wasn't sure she could do anything about carpets in landfills—no one in the company was talking about this kind of thing—but she knew the vice president of sales, who had access to the office of the CEO, a man named Ray Anderson. Joyce mailed a copy of Hawken's book to the VP and asked him to put it on the corner of Ray's desk that was always kept clear.

Ray read the book and saw the problems with his "take-make-waste" business model. As a result, he became one of the first and most vocal corporate executives to make the environment his focus. Ray Anderson's writing, speaking, and action in his firm propelled the whole field of sustainable business forward.[3]

Joyce said, "I was trying to follow through with what I had promised to Melissa. I didn't have any strong feeling that it was going to make any difference." We rarely know where our conversations will lead and it may be decades if you ever come to know the results.

We also encounter people who do not want to see themselves as activists or organizers working toward a societal transformation. You may want to work on a smaller scale, nudging habits and behaviors in your immediate family or team so people can be healthier and more responsible. You may simply want to "be the change" through your own actions. Our experience, however, is that each of these routes for action still requires conversation. You will have conversations with your office mates or family members about what you are doing. You will ask people for moral support. You will want to share what you've done so as to inspire others. Only when we make these conversations effective can we achieve our goals. And as we'll explore, you will also have conversations with yourself along the way.

The following chapters are about how all those conversations go—conversations about the future we are heading into and the future we want to create.

Too often we avoid these conversations or we give up on them because we just know they are going to go awry. At some point you might have gotten into a political sparring match over an otherwise friendly dinner table and learned that some issues appear to be too contentious to discuss. We may want to engage with our colleagues, neighbors, spouse, parents, and in-laws about the issues that matter to us, but we fear our efforts will be futile. We all hear and say things like "That's why I've learned not to talk politics at family gatherings," "That's why I don't talk about my values with my colleagues." When issues get polarized, we protect ourselves from getting zapped.

The irony is that this challenge is one that we share with our friends and relatives on all sides of the political spectrum. Whether we prefer to tune into Fox News and Glenn Beck or we're in the NPR and Democracy Now! crowd, the other camp seems absurd and too distant for us to reach.

In our experience, polarization is not a matter of how far left or right your ideologies are. Polarization is the breakdown in healthy communication or dialogue that includes divergent values.

Even our own organizations contain subgroups—one more concerned with social impact and another more concerned with financial performance. If we try to engage across these lines, the conversations often don't go the way we want. More often, we simply avoid the conversations altogether. Whether we've crashed and burned or sidestepped a difficult conversation entirely, we're left with the same result. We're stuck in a place where the only people we're engaging with are those who already agree with us. We continue "preaching to the choir" in an echo chamber of like-minded friends and online social networks.[4]

With big, pressing issues, this won't be enough. We're not going to end poverty or human rights violations by talking among social justice advocates. Similarly, we're not going to solve global climate change, habitat loss, or water pollution by rallying only the tried-and-true environmental activists. And we're not going to solve obesity without reaching outside the circle of public health advocates. All of these challenges require big changes—from new personal habits to innovation to shifts in public policy. They require constituencies of supporters far greater than what we have now. And yet we so often find ourselves falling short. It seems so hard to effectively share what's most important to us in conversations that could make a difference.

The purpose of this book is to create a new set of possibilities. By harnessing the power of conversation, we can break through gridlock and turn polarization into useful energy to accomplish our goals.

Start where you are

How do we take these big-picture issues of gridlock and polarization down to the level of one-on-one conversations between people? We look for where we personally have gotten stuck.

First, let's define "being stuck." It means taking (or avoiding) action repeatedly without achieving our stated goals.

We don't always notice when we're stuck. The first time our default strategy doesn't work, we might decide to try again or try harder. In a conversation, we'll repeat ourselves or attempt to explain ourselves. Then, maybe we adapt our approach, using slightly different words. We may bring in outside sources, facts, and perspectives. We may continue on a number of iterations, thinking, "Why don't they get it?" Or we may point the finger at ourselves and think, "What else can I do to get through to them?"

At some point in this journey, we may become resigned. We may decide that our goals just aren't worth pursuing—or at least not with the people we're talking with. You may say to yourself, "It's time to move on."

If that were really the case, we don't think you would have read this far into the book. Admit it: you care. We think you are reading this book because you share some goals with us and with your fellow readers:

- We want to take action in our own lives or engage others to produce some common good.
- We want people and other life to thrive around us.
- We want ourselves to thrive.

Being stuck means that we are repeatedly having a conversation, or repeatedly avoiding a conversation, and yet we are not achieving our goals. Instead, we are creating the following costs and consequences:

- We give up on our own power to take action.
- We fail to engage or inspire people, or worse, we inspire active resistance.
- We leave people suffering around us rather than flourishing.
- We diminish rather than strengthen relationships.

Does this mean we are bad, terrible, awful people? Of course not. We're just stuck.

Our goal is to help you be more *effective*—to define results that are meaningful to you and to achieve them. To do that, we'll start by reflecting on the specific situations where we find ourselves stuck. We will ask you to choose one conversation from among those you listed in exercise 1 and reflect on it a bit more.

Focus on real, live conversations

A quick word of warning: Whenever people come to us to learn how to be more effective advocates and leaders, we ask them to reflect on a conversation that is stuck. Some people have a very specific conversation that's important to them and they come straight out with it. Many people, however, instantly transform into masters of avoidance. We are each artfully skilled at avoiding real conversations that matter in real life.

To avoid reflecting on a specific conversation with a specific person, you might be tempted to refer to a group or class of people—for example, "When I talk to management . . ." You might effortlessly create a theoretical conversation that has never actually happened but speak about it as though it's real—for example, "If I were to speak to Governor [of a state I've never been to] . . . "

In our workshops, we've seen people talk about a specific conversation with a specific person for twenty minutes before they reveal that the person is dead or left the company years ago or is otherwise no longer a part of their lives. If you've met people only in passing, never got their names and could not find them again if you wanted to, these are not powerful conversations to work on. They're unreal, or at a minimum, they are not "live" examples. These are decoys or diversions from doing the difficult work of taking on real conversations that matter to you. Keep it real.

Exercise 2
Identify stuck conversations

Part A: Conversations that have gone off the rails

Choose a real conversation about improving the world that didn't go the way you wanted it to go. Perhaps you simply did not achieve your goals. Perhaps you found yourself feeling unsettled afterward about where you left the conversation or relationship. Start by looking at list 2 from exercise 1, but choose a real conversation.

Real conversations

- Are with a specific person who has a name.
- Have a history of dialogue in a specific place and time.
- Are current. You think about them. The person is living and still in your life. You see (or actively avoid) the person. You have the power to contact the person (or know someone who can connect you).
- Are important to you. They matter. Producing new results is worth the work of reflection.

In your notebook, answer the following questions about a real conversation:

- Who is the person this conversation is with?
- What is the person's relationship to you?
- Why does the conversation matter to you?
- What do you want to accomplish?
- When and where has the conversation taken place?
- What has been said in the conversation so far? Write out the conversation. Note that our recollection is often biased and incomplete. It can help to close your eyes, visualize,

and listen again, as specifically as possible, for what you said and heard verbatim.

This exercise is essential because it is the basis of all the reflection work we will ask you to do.

If you have several examples in mind, you can repeat this exercise, identifying a few specific conversations that have gone off the rails. If you consider skipping writing down one conversation because you have many in mind, then refer back to our earlier warning on being masters of avoidance.

Part B: Conversations that never happen

In part A, we invited you to consider conversations that didn't go the way you wanted them to go. These are memorable, but they are not the whole story. We also asked you to recall *avoided conversations* in exercise 1, list 3.

Consider that you avoid *far more* conversations that you're concerned won't go well. And your ability to avoid saying anything risky is so profoundly developed, you don't even remember the vast majority of the conversations you've avoided. You're swimming in these conversations, like a fish swims in water, and you typically never see them.

Right now, and over the next week, take note of the conversations you avoid. You might carry a small notebook with you, use the voice-recorder on your phone, or jot yourself an e-mail so that you can note it immediately.

For example, let's say you care about the health of the oceans and farms that produce your food. Sometimes you ask questions like, "Where was this fish caught?" or "Is this organic?" Now notice where you don't ask these questions. Chances are, you ask

Continued on next page

them where people or establishments are likely to have a well-developed answer and avoid asking them in places where the conversation might be less comfortable (but where it could actually make a difference!).

Notice when you see people take actions that you believe create negative impacts (e.g., making a sexist comment, littering) or they miss an opportunity where you think they could have generated a positive impact. When have you made it a topic of conversation with them, and when have you avoided it?

When you're in the presence of particular groups of people, when do and don't you raise the issues that matter to you?

Notice if there are friends or family members with whom you often discuss politics and others with whom you avoid discussing politics.

Replace "politics" in the previous sentence with any topic that is meaningful to you. That could be "spirituality," "parenting," or "your work," for example. With whom do you talk about what's most meaningful to you? With whom don't you talk about what's most meaningful?

Once you have a collection of these avoided conversations, choose one that seems important, and answer the questions from part A as they relate to the selected conversation you are avoiding.

Our goal is to help you look at these stuck conversations and get them unstuck by supporting *authentic conversations*. To clarify why that might be the right approach for you, we will first consider the alternative strategies, which we group into two categories: *power plays* and *framing*.

Power plays can't help you strengthen relationships

A number of strategies that might occur to us in stuck conversations could be labeled as "power plays." These are things to say and do that could help you achieve your goals without having to engage deeply with your opponent. These include the following:

- Going around the person by talking to other influential people in the situation or going over the person's head
- Redirecting money or other incentives to coerce the person
- Waiting until the person is no longer in a position of influence or the issue becomes irrelevant
- Picking your battles—letting one issue drop to free up time, resources, and political capital to work on another
- Exiting the situation because you don't see any possibility for change

We can't cover all these strategies thoroughly in this book. If they seem like the right fit for your situation, other books can help you navigate power and politics in this way.[5]

But what if you think those methods won't apply well to your situations or they are inadequate to fulfill your goals? Ask yourself whether any of the following apply:

- You don't have power at your disposal; you lack resources or authority.
- You do not want to disempower the person.
- You do not want to exit: the issue is important or urgent.
- You want to share your values such that they inspire others.
- You simply care about the person a great deal.
- You are looking for something greater that could emerge out of a creative dialogue.
- You hold a minority view or you want to inspire others to join your cause.

If your situation fits some of these criteria, then you are probably interested in a different approach. You may want to keep the power and influence strategies in your back pocket as your backup,[6] but you'd prefer a way of engaging that could strengthen your relationship and produce more optimal results.

Framing breaks down in unfamiliar and polarized situations

The next set of options you are likely to encounter are more subtle forms of influence, which also have their pros and cons. We'll call these "framing" or "translation" strategies. For example, many books and consultants tell us to make the business case for diversity or sustainability or social responsibility. They argue that making our organizations friendlier to women, ethnic minorities, and LGBT communities will increase the quality of our talent pool. They ask us to show how going "green" can be "gold" by reducing costs.[7] They explain how social responsibility can increase employee engagement or loyalty.

Many of these ideas trace back to linguist George Lakoff, who examines the language and ideas behind political movements.[8] He suggests that we should use "frames" and metaphors that make our goals appear to fit with others' values. We should speak the other person's language. These strategies are useful and an essential piece of the puzzle.

Here is an example of what we mean by framing. John Frey from Hewlett Packard Enterprise (HPE) was a workshop participant whom we interviewed for this book. He works on sustainability strategy and is in charge of engaging with HPE's customers to help them advance their social and environmental performance through the use of HPE solutions. In the early days, he would get invited to customer presentations to talk about his own company's work on these issues. He would share HPE's philanthropic work and efforts at reducing their carbon footprint in the hope that HPE's internal efforts might inspire their customers.

> I'm having these conversations, and I'm recognizing that people are starting to zone out. They're starting to do e-mail. They're starting to almost go to sleep. I'm thinking to myself as I'm presenting this slide deck, in real time, "What the heck is going on here? How do we have such a big miss?" Clearly, I'm passionate . . . [but]

> why can't I get them excited about something that I'm
> excited about? That was sort of an "aha!" moment for
> me, to take a step back and say, I'm speaking English
> to someone that only speaks French—no great surprise
> they're not very engaged.

This experience prompted John to reconsider his approach. He began sitting in on full days of customer briefings to better understand customers' particular challenges. He asked questions and listened. And he worked to frame his messaging in terms of his customers' specific needs.

> As I started doing that, people started paying attention.
> . . . We are not only talking their language, but I'll refer
> to their business plans and say, "Your business plan says
> you have this challenge, so let me talk to you a little bit
> about how I can help you do that." . . . There's a much
> deeper level of connection and credibility that enables
> me to provide value to them for things that they had
> never connected to sustainability.

Throughout the book you will see great examples of people doing this kind of translation work. You can study and mimic what works for them. John has trained an entire department to "get past sustainability speak" and use the language and branding he's created for what HPE calls "Efficient IT."

The framing approach may work well for you, and we encourage you to try it. However, we have seen four ways that the translation and framing approach repeatedly runs into trouble, particularly when issues have gotten polarized and stuck. As a result, we revisit the idea of framing in chapters 5 and 7 but did not make it the focus of this book.

The first trouble occurs when we are reframing our agenda as a way to meet others' goals, but *we don't really care that much about their goals.* For example, we know we *should* frame energy efficiency as a short-term cost savings, but what we are actually passionate about is the chance to prevent climate change. When this happens, the agenda can feel false and it can be beyond challenging to say the right words in the right frame in real time.

Second, others may not buy your carefully framed argument because they suspect there is something you are not saying. *They may have a background of mistrust* for your primary motivations or those of your group. People often notice when they are being manipulated.

Third, when others push back on our carefully framed arguments, *we get frustrated.* We find ourselves in a heated debate, or we avoid a conversation entirely because we fear we might. We often retreat to our well-worn habit of preaching to the choir about how "they don't get it."

The fourth issue is that we may not know which frame to use because no one has done this particular translation before. We might think we know what Democrats, Republicans, or chief financial officers in general care about. But we haven't done the research. We haven't shared deep conversations with them. Or our attempt may fall flat because we haven't yet developed a frame or translation that is specific to this organization and this person in this situation.

The intention of this book is *not* to help you create a script with talking points in response to every argument. As we said in the preface, getting a stuck conversation unstuck is not about finding "the right thing to say" but about making a fundamental shift in who we are *being*, freeing ourselves up for a creative and authentic new approach.

Start with authenticity

A key step in this journey is to develop a new perspective on authenticity. When we connect with others in authentic conversations, we can make progress toward a better world—a world beyond what we ever thought possible. Getting there, however, requires confronting the key sources of *inauthenticity* that drive conversations into patterns of predictable pitfalls. We organized this book to help you navigate pathways through otherwise hazardous terrain.

We go into depth about authenticity in chapter 2. Most of the time, people use "authentic" to describe when a person is acting consistently with the past. Unfortunately, this idea gets us stuck. It roots people in predictable patterns, re-creating the divisions and conflicts of the past. We help you experience a new notion of authenticity, one based on matching who we are with the future we want to create. To break the pattern, we come clean with others and ourselves about the ways we have been inauthentic. We can then generate new conversations that are aligned with our values. The subsequent five chapters take you through a series of steps to do just that.

What's possible

Imagine if activists and advocates were seen as being authentic, honest, moving, open, inspiring, powerful, kind, and compassionate. We think a whole new discourse is possible in movements toward social and environmental change. Our movements can become a source of flourishing for the people involved—on the way toward the flourishing of all life. As that happens, our efforts will be inviting and expansive and will grow to the quality and scale needed to create the world we want.

Along the way, we will improve our relationships with the people who matter most in our lives. Those expanded relationships will create the foundation on which we can effect change and will be a source of our own vitality. That is a surprising result we often see in our work. We have observed how some healing and growth can provide much-needed nourishment for the tireless advocate.

The starting point is your own reflection. As we said in the introduction, this book will be a journey. Each chapter will be an experiential inquiry, inviting you to explore, unpack, and transform the conversations that matter to you. Provided you take on the exercises, you'll soon be harnessing the power of conversation.

chapter 1 summary

- We have a profound lack of consensus about the nature of the world's problems or what to do about solving them.

- Every formula for action and problem solving has one thing in common: having conversations with people.

- Conversations about big issues often get stuck. Being stuck means taking or avoiding action repeatedly without achieving our stated goals. When we care about something and we're stuck, there are consequences.

- Other approaches to stuck issues and conversations include power plays and framing or translation. Our book explores the power and possibility of *authentic conversations* to create a better world.

- *Do the work*: Choose one real, live conversation for further reflection and exploration in the chapters ahead.

2

(In)Authenticity
The key to getting unstuck

We take a big risk by placing authenticity at the center of our exploration because our popular culture uses the word to mean so many different things. As one reader said, "When both Pope Francis and Donald Trump can be described by admiring fans as 'authentic,' I don't know what the word means anymore."

Pause here and make some notes as you consider this question: What does an authentic conversation look like to you?

- - - ◗ -

Exercise 3
What does authenticity mean to you?

Which people in your life would you identify as being authentic and why?

What specifically have they said or done that you relate to as being authentic? Inauthentic?

What would you say makes a conversation authentic?

What specifically have you said or done that you relate to as being authentic? Inauthentic?

What most people call "authenticity" is the tendency to speak our mind, take a clear position, and be consistent with what we've said and done before. As activists, we were taught that being authentic means being certain, persistent, and unapologetic. If we feel any degree of ambivalence or uncertainty, we just stay quiet.

The need to be certain can make for entertaining television debates, but it is limiting too. It creates unproductive friction in our relationships while eliminating opportunities for dialogue, learning, or innovation. On the wider stage, it creates polarization among the loudest activists with most of us remaining silent.

This kind of authenticity is grounded in *consistency with the past*. In fact, the first definition of "authentic" in the Oxford dictionary uses the words "made or done in the traditional or original way, or in a way that faithfully resembles an original." So we assume "authentic" people act in a way that is consistent with how we have seen them act, what we have heard them say, or "their roots."[1] This can be good. You make a commitment that you will stand up for a community, organization, or ideal, and you stick to it. People know what to expect. They can rely on you. You honor your word. In this sense, consistency with the past can be important in maintaining your integrity and existing relationships.

Consistency with the past can lead to getting stuck

The trouble is that consistency with the past can hold you back from creating a new future. It gets you stuck in repetitive patterns of conversation or behavior. How often have you found yourself in a debate about issues and heard yourself saying the exact same phrases and telling the exact same stories you have before? If you consider where your 'talking points" come from, you'll find that you are recycling conversations from the past. They might come from a parent or older sibling, a friend or colleague, an article you read, or a public figure you heard. This is one factor that causes polarization and gridlock to persist.

What happens if you have new experiences, learn new information, and meet people who challenge your point of view? In that circumstance, holding onto the past stops being true self-expression. Or what if you find that the conversations you've been having aren't producing the results you want? Maybe they are insufficient or even incompatible with the future you want to create. Then consistency with the past can be harmful to your cause.

Put simply, a past-based definition is frozen, or *static*. Let's set static authenticity aside for a moment and think about *dynamic* authenticity.

Dynamic authenticity is aligned with the future

You might be asking, who are we (Jason and Gabriel) to tell you how to be authentic? We are bundles of conflicting attitudes and desires. We want long-term solutions, *and* we want them now. We want everyone on Earth to flourish, *and* we would like to boot litterers off the planet. We want social equity, *and* we want to be independently wealthy. We want to act with self-determination, *and* we want to be coerced *and* rewarded into doing the right thing. We want people to stop driving their unnecessarily large vehicles, *and* we treasure our dogs, who have a large carbon footprint (from their meat-based, processed-food diet).[2]

If you found yourself chuckling as you read that last paragraph, or if we seem a little more human for admitting our contradictions, you are noticing a fundamental premise of our work. When we express these inconsistencies—our own inner conflicts that usually remain hidden—we create a different kind of space. We expose our vulnerability, our journey of growth. Our own inner tensions make the conversation come alive.

Surprisingly, it's not that difficult. We are humans, and we are complicated. We all have a profound capacity for love, awareness, and courage. We are also deeply motivated to stay safe and to look good. We will avoid hard work, yet we'll climb mountains for fun. We judge others for being judgmental. We strive to win, dominate, and control, and we like to belong, to be heard, and to be loved.

It turns out that where people are thriving and innovating together across "party lines," a different kind of authenticity is at work—one that is dynamic and alive (table 1). Rather than being true to the person you've known yourself to be, imagine being true to your growth, not knowing who you could become.[3] Rather than being consistent with the past, imagine being consistent with a future you really want. Imagine riding waves of continual inquiry rather than anchoring in certainty. Imagine connecting with people, whether or not you have always agreed, based on your common humanity and the future you could create together. This idea of dynamic authenticity is more like the Oxford dictionary's third definition of "authentic": "(in existentialist philosophy) relating to or denoting an emotionally appropriate, significant, purposive, and responsible mode of human life."[4]

Table 1 Static authenticity versus dynamic authenticity

Static authenticity	Dynamic authenticity
Speaking my mind and opinions	Sharing my personal story and the perspectives that arise from it (knowing they are likely to change)
Consistency with the past	Aligning with the future you want
Consistency in all statements; anchoring in core, permanent self	Anchoring in process of learning, discovery, and growth
Polarized certainty	Owning ambivalence, creative tension, exploring uncertainty
Imperviousness: immunity to influence and criticism of others	Vulnerability and openness to learning
No apologies	Acknowledging where we are out of alignment with who we want to be

For the purposes of this book, we can work with the following definition:

> "Authenticity" means striving to be consistent with the world you want to create and being honest about your inconsistencies.

Notice how you respond to this new idea. When you start to consider being oriented toward growth, toward the future that is inherently unknown, how does that feel? When you imagine people expressing ambivalence and vulnerability and acknowledging their inauthenticity, how does that feel? On one hand, you may be enlivened by the idea, inspired, excited.

At the same time, the uncertainty could be terrifying. When we think of authenticity as static, being authentic means knowing who you are. Dynamic authenticity involves not knowing who you are or who you could become. As humans, we're often uncomfortable with ambiguity or uncertainty, so you may actively avoid those experiences. It's okay if this idea is uncomfortable or disconcerting. Think of that discomfort as a healthy sign of your experience of being alive. Discomfort is a part of growth and venturing into the unknown.

Exercise 4
What does authenticity mean to you? (continued)

Flip back to exercise 3 and reflect on your own notions of authenticity.

Which of the characteristics that you wrote down are pointing to the past?

Did you mention being true, real, or consistent? If so, true to what? Real according to what? Consistent with what? Did you say authenticity is in accordance with the original? True to who you knew yourself to be?

These are typical dictionary meanings of "authenticity" and they're all pointing to the past.

Now consider the idea of *dynamic authenticity*. Is it enticing? Uncomfortable? Both?

Reflect on a time when you spoke your mind and opinions but didn't get the result you wanted. What might it have been like to share your story, your contingent perspective, knowing you didn't have all the information, knowing your opinions will change as you learn and grow?

What would it be like to tell your story, the story of who you are, knowing even your account of your own past will change as you learn and grow?

Who in your life would you identify as being dynamically authentic and why?

Is there a specific recent conversation you recall that you now experience as having expressed dynamic authenticity? What exactly was said and who said it? What was your experience of the conversation during and afterward?

The cornerstone of dynamic authenticity is a key paradox that we will explore and experience in this book: *the pathway to authenticity is to acknowledge our inconsistencies.* If authenticity is about aligning with the future you want, one opportunity for growth is to find the misalignments.

Dynamic authenticity is a team sport

In the next several chapters we will take you through that process of identifying inconsistencies. We will ask you to consider those contexts where you have worked to engage people in the issues that matter to you. We will ask about the times when your actions, your words, your *way of being* have fallen out of step with your aspirations. What can those occasions reveal about your own inner contradictions that have yet to see the light of day? In identifying these moments of *inauthenticity*, we create an opportunity to express ourselves more fully and powerfully.[5]

When we do, something different becomes possible. Instead of keeping us separate from other people, our hidden selves bring us closer! We laugh about our shared imperfections and just how mixed up we really are. From there we can create the space for something new—a fresh authentic conversation toward a better world.

Playing this game alone, however, is very difficult because often we can't see our inconsistencies without help. In the introduction we described this book as "serious play," and it is a team sport. It requires getting help from our friends to reflect—to hold up a mirror and help us see how we have approached challenging conversations.

If you haven't chosen someone already, we strongly suggest you invite a friend, a colleague, or a group of people to join you as you work through this book. Invite someone to be your coach. Find someone who can quickly see the traps you fall into, isn't afraid to say so, and can help guide you along this journey. Your coach may even agree to join you! You can commit together to help each other break through gridlock, however that may appear in each of your lives.

Our experience is that authenticity grows in conversation. We plant the seed with our own commitment to producing new results. We lay down roots in these peer-support "buddy" relationships, where we get to explore and be vulnerable. Then we reach out into the open air, newly approaching difficult conversations. If we are persistent, we get to enjoy the fruits of new understanding and creative outcomes.

- -

Exercise 5
Choose a buddy

First, make a short list of people whom you think would be fun to include on your journey through this book. Consider the following:

- Who is willing to listen to you about the issues and problems you care about in the world, even if they don't always agree with the way you go about trying to solve them?

- Whom are you willing to listen to?

- Whom would you trust to hear the details of situations where you have gotten stuck or fallen on your face?

- Who will tell you what others may be afraid to tell you? Who is not afraid to confront you with what they think about your attitude and actions? Who is willing to challenge your interpretation of events? Who recommended this book?

Continued on next page

- Who is separate enough from the context of your challenges that they can help you think through them dispassionately? (For example, if you are trying to make changes at home, think twice before picking your spouse; if you are trying to make changes at work, think twice before picking your boss.)

- Who else may benefit from learning how to harness the power of conversation in a polarized world?

Next, choose one or more partners, share this book with them, and ask them to play along. For example, you could tell them you want to get better at talking about tough issues you care about and you would like their help and peer coaching.

Then, create your own set of agreements for how you'll best support one another along this journey. Here are some ideas:

- Be candid and challenge one another. If you hear your buddy say something that sounds off or unfair or makes unquestioned assumptions, then pause the person and point it out.

- Hold each other accountable. If you hear your buddy theorize or complain but avoid taking action, encourage the person to make a real move. Create a deadline together.

- Be compassionate *and* persistent. If you sense you or your buddy is feeling frustrated or resigned, take a break. But instead of just dropping the conversation, return to it while trying something new.

We recommend your list of agreements be explicit yet not fixed. You can always come back and add to it or amend it as you learn.

chapter 2 summary

- Most of the time, the word "authentic" is used to describe when people are acting consistently with their past beliefs, statements, behaviors, and cultural identity. This common idea of authenticity is static and can solidify gridlock and polarization.

- Rather than being consistent with the past, we invite you to be consistent with a future you really want and to embark on a process of learning and growth. We call this "dynamic authenticity."

- The key to dynamic authenticity is being honest and vulnerable about our inconsistencies and contradictions. It is often easiest to do this in trusting relationships and then to expand from there.

- *Do the work*: Invite a friend, colleague, or a group of people to join you as you work through this book. Find someone who can quickly see the traps you fall into and isn't afraid to say so. Invite the person to be your coach, and offer to reciprocate.

3

Know What You Bring
The hidden baggage of conversations

Over and over in our own experience, in our interviews with advocates, and in workshops with aspiring leaders, we see a recurring pattern. When we get fired up about issues that matter to us, we approach our conversations in a particular way.

Here's a story from Jason's experience:

> Heading into the basement to grab something in our storage room, I notice that the lights are on. I grumble, flick the switch, and then head upstairs to the kitchen, where my wife is doing dishes. "Someone left the lights on in the basement," I proclaim, arms crossed.

Freeze-frame. What is going on in this situation? What Jason has described here is the first moment of a conversation. He has conveyed things that you would see and hear on a video recording. Reading his description, you might infer a great deal about the hidden conversation he is having with himself: "What a waste of electricity (and money and carbon). Someone (not me!) has left the lights on. I better figure out who it was and teach them why this is bad so they don't do it again. I always have to be the guardian of green in this house." All of this is bundled up in the simple statement he has made—and he acts as if his wife doesn't know it!

> My wife immediately counters with a wry smile, "Well, 'someone' leaves the light on in the shower every morning. And you know what? I just turn it off."

How does she see what's going on here? What gives her a window into the hidden conversation in Jason's head? Part of it is that they've been married more than a decade, these are well-worn patterns, and she can anticipate the lecture he's about to give her about energy conservation. He's created a pattern that she's projecting onto what he's saying now (and appropriately so!). But something else is present in that moment in his expression—a stance, a tone, the way he's phrased his statement. Somehow, by avoiding the language of blame, he still manages to create an implicit accusation.

Beyond the words he says, there is a way he is *being* in this situation: judgmental, self-righteous, and passive-aggressive. This way of being has two issues. The first is that it is unlikely to be effective toward engaging Jason's wife in conversation or ensuring the lights get turned off. At best, he provokes sarcasm and some gentle mocking of his own bad habits. At worst, he fires up an argument.

At a deeper level, being self-righteous is out of line with the world he wants to create. When Jason and his wife talk to their children about their values and expectations of them or he drafts a team charter for his organization, what does he stand for? He usually talks about pursuing humble mastery and compassion and care for people and nature. But then in these everyday situations, he shows up in a way that disrespects other people and sends conversations off the rails.

This is a wider issue for advocates on social, environmental, and political issues. We often show up being holier than thou, certain, dogmatic, or intellectually superior. We spend a lot of time telling others what they should and shouldn't do. We focus on the next possible apocalypse more than we do on the world we want to create. It's not very inviting, and it's frankly not a lot of fun. Nevertheless, we wonder why people aren't flocking to our cause. We retreat to our well-worn phrase, "They just don't get it." And we find ourselves frustrated and upset.

In this chapter we address the question, Are our ways of being aligned with the world we want to create?

Our way of being is tied with our background conversation

How can we see our way of being? A fish, swimming in water, is not aware of the water. In the same way, we are often not aware of our way of being and how it is shaping the way we act and the way others respond to us.

In the story above, Jason was not quite aware of his way of being in the moment. Two factors conspired to make him a little more aware after the fact—to the point where he could name his way of being. The first was that his wife noticed it. We can tell because she pointed out an alternative way of being in a similar situation: she suggested just being helpful and turning off the light (without the judgment and preaching). The second is that he took a moment to think back over the sequence of events and the thoughts running through his head along the way: he reflected.

The point is that noticing our way of being takes effort and self-effacing courage, and it is a profoundly important skill. Our way of being generates the set of things that we do (including what we say) and the things others do and say in response to us. Those actions and conversations give rise to the results we have in the world.[1] This process is shown in figure 1.

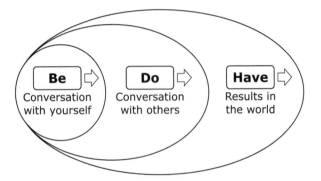

Figure 1 Our way of being gives rise to what we do and the results we have

In chapter 1 we shared a story about John Frey, at Hewlett Packard Enterprise, shifting his approach to be more effective at selling his company's sustainability services. The most powerful aspect of that story is not that he used a new *frame* to sell his company's services. What allowed him to generate that new frame is that he shifted his way of *being*.

He came to understand the effect his way of being was having on his audience. He was being passionate and proud about HPE's accomplishments in his presentations, but he saw that was leaving his customers disengaged. He shifted to a way of being that was *inquiring* and *connecting*. From there, a new set of ideas naturally came to him about how to interact with his customers. Doing followed being. He listened to their challenges, read their business plans, and helped them solve *their* problems. In doing so, he advanced his own organization's goals for business success and sustainability. He created a new language or conversation he could teach others.

Noticing our way of being is not trivial. It involves looking at how we are feeling internally and how we are coming across to others. It involves both introspection and empathy. Developmental psychologists say this kind of process is a key to personal growth—seeing what is hidden and going to work on it. It is the basis of our *becoming*—our journey toward greater awareness, consciousness, capability, and freedom. At the same time, it can be challenging and painful because it requires being vulnerable.[2]

So how can we come to understand, and ultimately shift, our way of being? In conversations with others, our way of being emerges from the background conversation we are having with ourselves. That ongoing conversation you're having with yourself influences the way you come across to others.

Stop reading for a moment and listen to the conversation you're having with yourself.

Stop. Listen.

You might be thinking, "A conversation with myself? I'm not having a conversation with myself. I don't need to do this step; I'll just keep reading." *That is the conversation we are talking about.*

It is the voice running in your head before, during, and after you talk with others. Different practices have different names for this voice. You may have heard people talk about reflecting on their "internal monologue" or "stream of consciousness," or they may refer to "observing the process." You have thoughts happening, and those thoughts can be described as a voice or voices.

The conversations you're having with yourself create your way of being. Our thoughts and feelings create an internal tone. That tone shapes the nonverbal and verbal dynamic of our conversations with others. And the way our conversations go—whether we successfully share our values and vision and plan of action—determines our results in the world. Once we notice the impact of our own way of being, then we start to free ourselves up. We can create new ways of being and start new conversations that produce new results. We enter into a process of becoming authentically aligned with our highest aspirations.

Our ways of being are shared

In this chapter and throughout this book we will help you access your way of being and the conversation with yourself. In doing so, we will make use of an important fact: as personal, intimate, and reflective as this inquiry may appear, it isn't really that personal.

Can you recognize yourself in Jason's story we shared above? Have you ever caught yourself being judgmental, self-righteous, or passive-aggressive? Chances are that you have. We're all human. We have inherited some ways of being. Some conversations with ourselves and others have been going on for a long time. We come to share these ways of being when we are born into a particular culture and when we join a broader discourse or movement, such as social justice or sustainability. Many of our pitfalls—traps that get us stuck—are commonly shared experiences in the pursuit of a better world. They can even become clichés. We find ourselves playing the activist who is strident and hot-headed or cynical and resigned.

We have conducted workshops in a variety of settings in different countries and with different communities. In our workshops, we ask participants to reflect on conversations that didn't go well or on conversations they were avoiding because of how they might go. Here are some examples of situations people have described:

- An employee wants to approach the chief financial officer of the company about the need to invest in social or environmental outcomes.

- A woman tries to engage her mother on issues of gay rights.

- A person argues for his chosen career path, and the difference he wants to make in the world, to a skeptical parent or grandparent.

Conversations like these are important. They have the potential to inspire others to take action and to support us in pursuing goals that matter to us. Unfortunately, they too often get stuck in conflict, frustration, or resignation, many times before they even begin.

"What was your way of being in that conversation when it got stuck?" In our workshops we pose this question and collect the responses. Figure 2 shows what we have heard.

Figure 2 Ways of being when people are stuck[3]

Imagine sitting on a long plane ride next to someone described by the above word cloud. Would you want to chat, or would you be calling for headphones and pretending to take a nap? These words reveal an issue with *our own ways of being*—they correlate with our conversations not going well.

Now, take another look at the word cloud, and imagine getting into a conversation where this is how you are going to feel and how you are going to come across. Does that seem like fun? Probably not! So our tendency is to avoid the hard conversations, those with the possibility of engaging with people who aren't already aligned with our values. We don't want to find ourselves being this way, feeling the way it feels, and being perceived this way by others. So we avoid the difficult conversations and fall short of our goals for creating a better world.

This is all bad news and good news. It's bad news because *we are our own worst enemy* in these situations. Our way of being gets in the way of our achieving our goals. One Fortune 500 employee, upon seeing this word cloud, said with a self-effacing chuckle, "That looks like my performance review!" The good news is, our way of being is one place where we have real agency. If the conversation is a dance, then the way of being is the tune. If the conversation is stuck, you can start dancing to a new tune and sometimes, even often, people will follow. Our exercises in this book will help you get to that place.

Another aspect of the word cloud is the *strong commonality* among the words. A few ways of being come up time and time again: frustrated, defensive, resentful, self-righteous, passive-aggressive, resigned. Many of the other words are close correlates: defeated, pushy, superior, know-it-all. We interpret this commonality to mean that our ways of being are shared, possibly even contagious. They arise in a shared context of being stuck—we are operating in a gap between the world as it is and the world we want, and we're not moving forward.

Unfortunately, these ways of being help create people's expectations of us as advocates and activists. Psychology researcher Nadia Bashir and her colleagues at the University of Toronto recruited a representative sample of North Americans using an online survey tool. They asked participants to name traits characteristic of a "typical" activist from different movements. Table 2 shows the most frequently mentioned traits of a "typical" environmentalist.

Table 2   Thirty most frequently mentioned traits of a "typical" environmentalist[4]

"Typical" environmentalist

tree-hugger	overreactive	nontraditional
vegetarian	unfashionable	outdoorsy
hippie	self-righteous	forceful
liberal	educated	animal lover
unhygienic	drug user	intolerant
militant	hairy	helpful
eccentric	determined	democrat
activist	stupid	annoying
caring	intelligent	crazy
protester	zealous	irrational

You may chuckle when you read this list. You may see a bit of yourself or others you know. Our point is, this is not personal. There is an important resonance between the ways of being our workshop participants identify in their personal reflections and this broader cultural study of how advocates are perceived in the world.

This is actually good news. By identifying the gap between who we're being and the world we say we want to create, we break the pattern and create a space for something new. We will guide you through a conversation to transform your own ways of being, your relationships, and your social movement. We will change the world the only way it has ever been done—one conversation at a time.

Uncover your background conversations

We're now going to take you through a process of transforming a conversation. First, it's important that you not merely read along. Recall exercise 2, where we asked you to think of a conversation that didn't go the way you wanted or that you're avoiding entirely because you're afraid it won't go well. Pick one conversation for yourself that fulfills exercise 2 before moving ahead.

Let's say you've chosen a specific conversation and have identified the details (who, when, where, what was said, what wasn't said). Most likely, your default reaction is to ask, What should I have said? What should I say now? In this inquiry, we are asking something different.

Start by getting in touch with your *conversation with yourself*. If your conversation with someone went off the rails, what thoughts were you having before, during, and afterward? If you have gotten stuck by *avoiding* a conversation that matters, then all you have is a conversation with yourself!

Exercise 6
Our unspoken background conversation

Choose one of the conversations you identified and wrote out in exercise 2. This could be a conversation that didn't go the way you wanted or one that you have been avoiding. Make certain you're choosing a conversation that is *live* and that *matters*.

A conversation is *live* if it still feels unresolved or incomplete, even if some time has passed. It is with someone who is in your life, someone you'll continue to be in conversation with (not the person you saw on the bus whom you have never met and don't know how to find). It *matters* if you really want to achieve something. That goal could be a concrete outcome like a change of behavior, or it could be a higher quality relationship with the person.

If this is an avoided conversation, then imagine it happening—play the recording in your mind of how you think it would go.

Now reflect on that conversation as follows:

Write down the unspoken or background conversation—what you were (and are now) thinking and feeling but not saying out loud. Feelings are basic: mad, sad, glad, afraid, ashamed. To notice feelings, sense your body's signals, like a pounding heart or heat in the face. Thoughts are interpretations or judgments of the other person or the situation. Write down whatever you can remember going through your mind.

If your conversation is one that didn't go well, write down what you were thinking and feeling before, during, and after the interaction. If your conversation is one you have been avoiding, write out the background conversation you're having with yourself about that conversation that isn't taking place.

In our workshops, participants have shared these re-sponses when asked to share their unspoken background conversations:

- "You're too lazy to figure it out."
- "Resolving these issues is more important than being nice to you."
- "I can't believe how selfish you are."
- "There's no good way to have this conversation."
- "You're not telling the truth."
- "You just don't get it. You're not even interested in getting it. Your mind's made up. You don't care what I say."
- "You say you want it, but you're not willing to take the necessary steps."

It makes sense that we aren't saying these things aloud—if we did, the conversation might go further off the rails. At the same time, think back to Jason's con-versation with his wife about the basement lights. She knew what Jason was thinking. These background con-versations are no big secret. One reason is that we may have said these things out loud in the past. If so, they are hanging there in the space between us—an expectation of what we'll say. They also bleed through in the pres-ent through our nonverbal communication. Our back-ground conversation affects our stance and our tone—our way of being. Let's look into that.

Exercise 7
Identify your ways of being

Step back and look at the whole interaction that you wrote out in exercises 2 and 6. Consider your background conversation with yourself. How would you describe your way of being in this conversation? What adjectives would you use? How do you think you came across? If it's an avoided conversation, how do you think you would come across?

Another way to get at this is to imagine that someone who knows you really well—your spouse, best friend, sibling, parent, or child—could watch a video of the interaction. Imagine this person can anticipate what's going through your head. *How would the person describe your way of being?*

Hint: You need not reinvent the wheel. Look back at the word cloud (fig. 2) for ways of being that may express your way of being in this conversation.

Share your reflections with your buddy, and see if your buddy agrees with the way you have described your way of being.

We can't emphasize enough the importance of stopping here and using exercises 2 and 6 to reflect. "How was I being?" is a much less familiar inquiry than "What should I do?" or "What should I have done?"

Stop.

Reflect: how would you characterize your way of being?

This inquiry may seem awkward. So give yourself the space to ponder and struggle with this a little. Set the book down and come back to it when you've developed your first, second, or third response.

Also, check in with your buddy. Have they named their way of being? Be candid. Don't hesitate to challenge them if they're trying to make it sound rosier than it is.

Part of the reason this exercise can be challenging is our tendency toward self-judgment: "I already beat myself up for the outcome of the conversation. Now you want me to confess to a way of being I'm not proud of?"

We are not asking, Are these ways of being good or bad? In fact, it's powerful *not* to label them as good or bad, right or wrong. They just are what they are. Judging ourselves for being judgmental is just more judgment. The more fruitful questions are: Do you find these ways of being effective? Are they authentic to the person you want to be and to the interaction and world you want to create? If the answer is no, then we want you to have the freedom to try something new.

Now that you've wrestled with that exercise, we will share some common challenges to identifying your way of being and tricks for overcoming them.

Ways of being can be tricky to see

We worked with one woman whom we'll call Alice. She shared that she was avoiding conversations with her mother because of issues around gay rights. She said, "My mother calls about every four months, it always blows up, and I ignore her calls for another four months. I've organized my whole life around social justice. I can't be true to my values and love my mother. She hates gay people."

We asked Alice to reflect on her way of being, and she got stuck and asked for help. She said, "I suppose I'm being optimistic." When we asked her to elaborate, she said, "I suppose I'm being optimistic that my mother can change."

We responded, "How would your mother describe your way of being? Would she describe you as being optimistic?"

After a pause, Alice said, "No, she'd describe me as being self-righteous and judgmental."

A couple of things are going on here. First, notice Alice's tendency to cover up, mask, or hide her way of being when recounting her conversations. Like Alice, we often won't say exactly what was said or what we were thinking because it's far from flattering. Rather, we'll give our summary of it. Recall Jason's story about the lights in the basement: "I grumble, flick the switch, and then head upstairs to the kitchen, where my wife is doing dishes. 'Someone left the lights on in the basement,' I proclaim, arms crossed."

What if Jason told the story this way: "I reached the top of the stairs and told my wife the lights had been left on." This latter description is still accurate and valid, yet it carefully strips out his way of being in that situation.

We've all mastered retelling stories in a way that strips out the ways of being that we're not proud of or that weren't effective. In our recounting, we carefully cover up the communications, verbal and nonverbal, that ran our conversation off the rails. Recounting the story this way leaves you looking good and the other person less so, but it doesn't give you access to transforming your conversation going forward.

Details matter. See how closely you can identify the verbatim conversation, what exactly was said and what wasn't said, that generated your way of being. Consider that your first responses may be a cover-up or mask hiding your actual way of being in the conversation.

Exercise 8
The spoken conversation

Go back to the spoken conversation you described earlier. Now that you have reflected on your background conversation and way of being, ask yourself, How well did I describe *everything* that was said and *how* it was said? Are you able to distinguish better what actually happened and remember things more clearly?

On a piece of paper or in your notebook, write down, as precisely as you can remember, a transcript of *what was said* and *visible actions taken*. If someone had a recording device, what would that person have seen and transcribed? That transcript could look like this:

Me: "＿＿＿＿＿"

Other person: "＿＿＿＿＿"

Me: "＿＿＿＿"

. . .

Is being in the eye of the beholder?

One question comes up frequently in our workshops at this point as we inquire into our ways of being in our conversations. Whose truth is the "true" truth? Whose perspective is the right one? If I think I'm being "optimistic" and the other person thinks I'm being "judgmental," who is right? Aren't both perceptions correct?

The truth is, how *you* think you're being makes little difference to the trajectory of the conversation. We invite you to *take responsibility for your way of being as perceived by the other person*. That's the one that counts. This is a powerful starting point because it puts the onus on you to show up the way you want to be perceived.

By looking at their conversation from her mother's perspective, Alice saw, "In reacting to my mother's righteousness and judgment, I become righteous and judgmental." Then Alice's righteousness and judgment might have generated more of the same in her mother, resulting in a downward spiral. Seeing this helped Alice free herself to create a new way of being and to approach the relationship with her mother in a new way.

Take a moment to explore your conversation from the perspective of the other person. What is your way of being? Will you take responsibility and own that way of being? Is there convergence between the two points of view? If not, keep looking. Examining and confronting your own contributions to the conversation's failure can be challenging. Paradoxically, the more confronting and uncomfortable it is, the more space you're creating for your own growth and breaking through gridlock in this specific conversation.

Being and inauthenticity

If you have a good handle on your way of being, we can confront the questions we raised earlier about authenticity. For you personally, is your own way of being aligned with your personal aspirations? Among your fellow advocates or in your movement, are the shared ways of being aligned with your shared purpose? For example, if you stand for compassion and inclusion, do you operate in compassionate and inclusive ways? As you try to engage broader constituencies in your companies, supply chains, marketplaces, families, schools, communities, and political parties, will your way of being help you succeed at inviting others to join your cause? Will they be inspired to change their behavior, invest resources, and endorse and vote on policies that improve the world in the way you say you want?

If you answer yes to these questions, great. Chuck the book and take a nap.

If the answer is no, you have successfully identified an important source of inauthenticity. You are beginning to create space for something new—a way of being aligned with your aspirations that naturally gives rise to the conversations and the world you want. Alice saw that she could be compassionate and loving, starting with her mother, and she would indeed be "true to her values."

First, however, we have to address a central puzzle. If and when we experience misalignment, why do we persist? Why do we sometimes get stuck in ways of being that fall short of producing the results we want? This is the question we address in the next chapter.

chapter 3 summary

- When we show up for a conversation with others, we carry the hidden baggage of background conversations with ourselves.

- We might try to mask our prejudices and assumptions about how the conversation will go, but they sneak through in the way we carry ourselves and the way we come across: our way of being. The conversation can get stuck before it even gets started.

- Our ways of being are shared, both in cultures of advocacy and in the basic human experience of difficult conversations. Our ways of being contribute to negative stereotypes and expectations of us as advocates.

- To get unstuck, we invite you to recognize whether your way of being is (dynamically) authentic. Is it consistent with achieving our immediate objectives? Is it in line with the world you want to create?

- *Do the work*: The next step in transforming conversations is to open up and confront this hidden baggage by getting in touch with your ways of being.
  - When your conversation got stuck, what were you thinking and feeling but not saying out loud?
  - What is your background conversation?
  - What was your way of being in that conversation when it got stuck?

4

Locate the Bait
What we gain when conversations lose

We'll begin this chapter with another story from Jason:

> When I came to MIT in 2005 to pursue a PhD, I joined a group of graduate student advocates. We put together a little manifesto about "what MIT should do" on sustainability, collected dozens of signatures from faculty, and handed them off to the administration. We asked for a meeting with the president of MIT so we could present our demands in person. We felt pretty cool.
>
> When we heard back from the president's office, however, we were told that they didn't know what to do with our proposal: we had no clear "asks," and they didn't know how to interpret what we were requesting.
>
> To be honest, we didn't know either, but it was easier to stew in frustration and demonize the administration. We decided that "they" didn't get it, weren't taking us seriously, and didn't really want to do what "they" should do.
>
> After the failed petition, our next approach was to push for an event with more focus: one in which we could force the administration to publicly commit to "walking the talk" and making the campus more energy efficient.

As we started planning the event, however, we ran into what felt like more roadblocks. At one point, I was in a conference room with fellow student advocates and university administrators. The conversation felt contentious—us pushing, them pushing back. They weren't willing to commit. I felt stuck.

What keeps conversations stuck? One way to describe this situation is that Jason and his friends encountered a *roadblock*—a barrier that someone else erected in their path, an obstacle to be broken down or overcome by force of will and political power. We ask ourselves questions like, How do we overcome resistance when people are blocking our efforts? Saul Alinsky's *Rules for Radicals* is a classic in this vein, assuming a powerful opponent and an insurgent group.[1]

We can, however, use a different metaphor, one that focuses on our own role in getting ourselves stuck. We have found it useful to think of stuck conversations as involving a pitfall, or a hidden trap. We stumble into it when we are on our journey to create a better world, with our particular background conversation and way of being. At the center of this metaphor is the bait in the trap, something so delicious that we grasp on tight. We enjoy the bait but bear the cost of being stuck.

The bait is the next fundamental source of inauthenticity we want to explore. Only when we identify the bait and let go of it, can we climb out of the trap and find a pathway around it.[2] Here's how it happened in Jason's story:

PITFALLS & PATHWAYS

BACKGROUND CONVERSATION   BEING   BAIT   THE FUTURE YOU WANT

COST OF BEING STUCK

In the conference room, Elsa Olivetti spoke up—she was a graduate student who had been at MIT for a few years. "It seems like your approach here is 'we think someone should do something.' My approach in these situations is usually 'we're here to help.'"

Her words affected me powerfully because I did experience her as positive and helpful. I stepped back, took a deep breath, and tried on that conversation with myself—"we're here to help."

I gulped and felt myself tense up at the prospect of a new approach. Taking on "we're here to help" would mean having to actually do the work. I might get over-loaded. I might fail to have a real impact. Of course, these were exactly the risks we had been asking the administration to take! In that moment, I saw just how much we had enjoyed feeling self-righteous and getting off easy.

At the same time, it was clear that our current approach was not helping us achieve our stated goals. We were stuck. So I took on "we're here to help" and let it guide my thinking and conversation. Almost immediately, the conversation shifted. We started asking questions instead of just arguing our points. We learned that graduate students around campus were quietly doing some very cool stuff that we could help boost. Our event ended up being the MIT Generator series, where students pitched hands-on projects on campus sustainability that we could execute together.

The response from the senior administration was powerfully supportive. Students spawned dozens of projects, and MIT took a few more steps on a long journey toward a comprehensive energy and climate change strategy.

Let's apply the pitfall metaphor to the MIT story. Jason was *stuck*, spending time in conversations without making any progress. His *background conversation* was, "I want the administration to take sustainability seriously, but they don't get it." Jason's way of *being* was self-righteous and frustrated. The *bait* was enjoying getting off easy, feeling like a righteous underdog, and placing the responsibility on the MIT administration. Jason got to feel certain that "we get it and they don't." Until he let go of that bait, there was no way to chart a new course. With his friend's help, he started to see a new *pathway*: "How can we be helpful and coordinate the great efforts of students, staff, and faculty toward a sustainable campus?"

Our goal is to help you identify your own pitfalls, but we recognize this can be tricky because so much is hidden. The cost of being stuck is buried beneath the brush. We may not even admit that there is a cost: we'll see our lack of progress as someone else's fault, a roadblock someone has put in our way. The problem does not seem to be a way of thinking that we have chosen—it appears to be the truth. The bait is often something we don't admit we want, either to others or to ourselves. Even if we see all this, it takes vulnerability to say that we have created our own trap. It takes even more courage to surrender the bait and face the risks of moving into unfamiliar territory.

The good news is that we all fall into pitfalls, and we often find a pileup in there! We can poke fun at ourselves when we realize we are all in this together. Jason and his fellow activists fell into a pattern we call "someone should." It takes a lot of forms: the government should, business should, my brother-in-law should; "they" should. It's such a tempting pitfall when complex issues and lots of relevant actors are involved. Claiming "someone should" allows us to pretend we're making a contribution while we're merely judging and criticizing others.

You got yourself stuck

The first step is to simply recognize when you are stuck and take responsibility for getting unstuck. "Stuck" is a relative term—we can only be stuck relative to where we want to go. Identifying pitfalls is about making you *effective* in reaching your goals.

Take a cold, clear look at the consequences of being stuck. What are you giving up in terms of your goals and aspirations? If you weren't stuck, where could you go? If you succeeded, what could be available for the world? These are costs of being stuck.

And there may be other costs, or *collateral damage*. When we create an atmosphere of disrespect, domination, or disillusionment, it can have lasting impacts on the vitality of our relationships. For example, we shared a story in the preface about Michaela, who had not eaten a meal with her mother in more than a year because of ongoing conflicts about obesity and unhealthy eating choices.

You may have an explicit goal to create flourishing around you. But if people are hurt, annoyed, or agitated by your approach, how likely are they to listen to your message? Are you creating relationships that will sustain you through your quest for a better world? Are you cultivating opportunities for others to be authentic around you?

Confronting the costs of being stuck is necessary if we are going to muster the courage and energy to take a clear look around and to get ourselves unstuck.

Exercise 9
The cost of being stuck

To identify the cost of being stuck, answer the following questions:

- How do you know you are stuck?
- What outcomes are you hoping to produce that you are not currently producing?
- What problem do you wish you could solve but can't?
- What goals and aspirations are you not realizing?
- What collateral damage might you be creating? How does your current way of being affect the people around you?
- How are you impacted emotionally and practically?

Pitfalls: Background conversations that get us stuck

The second step is to recognize that you are not the only one getting stuck and to look for patterns. As we pointed out in chapter 3, our ways of being are shared. The same is true of our background conversations, which we often inherit from others in our group, organization, or movement. Once we identify the conversations that get us stuck, we can flag them in our lives and avoid recurring pitfalls going forward. To help you in this analysis, we offer a table of pitfalls in the sustainability discourse. Your movement's pitfalls may be similar to these or more specific to your cause.

We have a few caveats:

- The pitfalls we identify in table 3 are not comprehensive. They're merely common examples drawn from our own recurring struggles and those of the people we've worked with.

- Pitfalls often occur together. One executive we worked with said that he skipped from one pitfall to another and to another, cycling and recycling through the pitfalls without moving forward.

- The pitfalls may not be perfectly accurate descriptions of your situation. The question is, can they point you toward your own background conversation and bait? Once you identify your own pitfalls, you have an opportunity to create a new conversation.

Table 3 A few common pitfalls

Pitfall	Example conversation	Cost of being stuck	Bait
Someone should	"Business should . . ." "The government should . . ." "China should . . ." "They should . . ." "I can't . . . I need a lot more money, power, connections before I can . . . ; therefore, they should."	Giving up of our own power and responsibility to make a difference	Getting off easy: holding a vision for how the world "should" be without taking ownership or responsibility for creating or realizing that vision

Pitfall	Example conversation	Cost of being stuck	Bait
Holier than thou	"I am more virtuous than you (because I recycle, bike, etc.)." "I see more than you (because I know the science, I see things from a systems perspective, etc.)." "I know what you want better than you do (because I read philosophical books about how to be happy)." "I'm not even going to have this conversation (because you don't get it, you don't care, or you do get it but you're distorting the truth for your own purposes)."	Loss of ability to engage and empower people beyond the choir Creation of "us versus them" perspective	Feeling right(eous), smart, superior, and certain that "I know the answer" in an uncertain world Dominating others, making them wrong

Continued on next page

Table 3 (*continued*)

Pitfall	Example conversation	Cost of being stuck	Bait
I know what progress is	"That's merely incremental change, and what we truly need is transformative change." "We are working on the biggest, noblest, and most important problem." "How dare you marine ecologists get in the way of my wind farm!"	Silos among groups of advocates: divided we fall Limited personal growth, less potential for learning from or engaging with others	Being right, making others wrong Being certain in an uncertain world Feeling justified personal importance or significance

Pitfall	Example conversation	Cost of being stuck	Bait
Lone wolf	"I am being the change." "They don't get it." "The system is wrong and I'm not a part of it." "This isn't my community."	Isolation, burnout Inability to inspire others or effect change	Feeling superior and righteous

Pitfall	Example conversation	Cost of being stuck	Bait
It's the right thing to do	"We should (buy greener products, recycle, turn off the lights) because it's the right thing to do." "Everyone is too focused on the costs and benefits when this is a moral issue."	Missed opportunities to design solutions that incorporate the diversity of values present within the community or organization Missed opportunities for sharing experiences of higher quality motivations	Feeling righteous Claiming the moral high ground Avoiding the hard work of seriously considering competing tensions

Pitfall	Example conversation	Cost of being stuck	Bait
Selfless OR selfish	"They're just in it to make a buck." "Those greedy people are the problem." OR "They don't understand business, we have to earn a living, and I don't want my kids to go without." "Those tree huggers live in a utopian la-la land."	Gridlock and paralysis Missed opportunities for collaboration Surrender of personal agency and responsibility to outside influences (e.g., the market)	Being right, making others wrong Being dependent on others to create economic value and earn money Avoiding envy for financial success Avoiding the challenging tensions of mission-driven business

Continued on next page

Table 3 (*continued*)

Pitfall	Example conversation	Cost of being stuck	Bait
Right now!	"The problems we face are too large and far too urgent to invest in education or waste time "building consensus." "What's most required is that we influence business and political leadership. They are the ones with the power to effect change."	Loss of staying power across generations Loss of authenticity: using short-term "crisis-based" strategies while advocating long-term thinking, advocating for equality that is inherently based on and perpetuates inequality, losing touch with those you're purporting to help	Creating urgency Exclusivity: chasing after and running with elites

Pitfall	Example conversation	Cost of being stuck	Bait
Humans OR nature	"Humans are the problem. There are too many of them." OR "Nature can take a backseat. Those spotted owl people need to pay attention to human suffering."	Loss of our ability to express our love for humans *and* other life Loss of our ability to share what we love with others Anthropocentrism or misanthropism	Feeling certain: simplifying the problem and having someone to blame

Pitfall	Example conversation	Cost of being stuck	Bait
Problem orientation	"This is wrong. Why is it this way?"	Focus on the past rather than the future	Being right about the way things are
	"This / that community / country / organization has so many problems."	Reactive rather than proactive, creative, transformative, or integrative conversations and behaviors	Having a simple focus for our attention amid a complex world
		Inability to see people's strengths and resources	Defining a clear enemy for directed anger

Exercise 10
Recognize pitfalls

Reflecting on common pitfalls is helpful if we want to uncover pathways toward being more effective in what matters to us.

From the table above, which pitfalls do you recognize in your own communities of friends, family, and colleagues?

Which pitfalls do you find yourself engaging in?

So why are these pitfalls so sticky? Why are these conversations popular when they don't produce the results we want? It's helpful to understand the bait if we want the freedom to avoid the pitfall.

Identifying the bait helps you get unstuck

A Sufi story tracing back to fourteenth-century central Asia, called "How to Catch Monkeys," illustrates this idea of bait. A hunter captures a monkey by placing a cherry in a bottle. The monkey reaches into the bottle and grasps the cherry, and his fist is too large to extract unless he lets go of the cherry. He will not let go, so he is trapped.[3] Videos on the Internet show a similar practice among African hunter-gatherers in the present day.[4]

In conversations about improving the world, the bait is not a cherry in a bottle. We are not literally in a trap. And yet the situation is the same: we grasp something rewarding, and we forget that we have a choice to let it go. What is that reward?

First, it is important to understand what the bait or reward is *not*. It is *not* achievement of our long-term objectives for a better future. It is *not* the satisfaction of a job well done. It is *not* delight in a healthy relationship that opens up new possibilities. These may be real commitments for you, and they may be exactly what you strive for in your advocacy. That is great. However, bait is about the *other* commitments you don't know you have that get you stuck in unproductive conversations.

Most bait is not "nice." As tempting as it is to say that we pursue only enlightened goals, the bait is usually something more ego focused. In our workshops, when reflecting on a specific conversation that got stuck, people often put forward a rosy picture of their bait as a first-pass reflection:

- "Knowing I've made a difference"
- "Saving time and being efficient"
- "Preserving my friendship"

Upon more reflection, each of these participants scratched beneath the surface. It turned out that "Knowing I've made a difference" was about being superior and dominating the other person. When they let that go, they created the space to be helpful and make a difference. "Saving time" was really about avoiding the vulnerability of difficult conversations. "Preserving friendship" was about staying safe from conflict; ironically, this was undermining a chance for intimacy.

In other words, if you complete the sentence "I want a better world but . . ." the bait is not the better world. It is not your stated objective. It is, as Robert Kegan and Lisa Lahey describe, a "hidden competing commitment."[5] The bait is concealed, nestled away in the framing of the problem and our way of being in that context.

When we coach people, understanding the bait is often the most challenging part of identifying a pitfall. This is partly because it's uncomfortable to confront. Saying we want one thing while also quietly wanting another is a very basic form of inauthenticity. The good news is that we've found that most forms of bait in conversations toward a better world can be distilled down to just four words: "right," "righteous," "certain," and "safe."[6] You can try them on to see what fits.

Bait usually involves right, righteous, certain, and safe

Let's explore these four basic kinds of bait.

Getting to be right is nice. We have spent every year of our schooling getting rewarded for knowing the right answer. Maybe we were the ones who got the gold stars, the good grades, and the approving nod from parent and teacher, and we felt secure and valued in the world. Or perhaps we never got those things, so it's all the more rewarding when we do get to feel right, smart, knowledgeable, and correct.

Feeling righteous is tasty as well. When we're the righteous ones, we get to (mis)quote Mahatma Gandhi: "Be the change you wish to see in the world." Often we'll make some kind of sacrifice: Stop eating red meat? Take a low-paying job at a nonprofit when all our buddies are going into finance? Now we're set! Of course, it's a lot easier to feel like a saint when we can point to a sinner. And we have plenty of bad guys to choose from.

Feeling certain is particularly cozy because being uncertain is so uncomfortable. If we're going to sacrifice red meat to be green, do we want to wonder whether vegetable-based meat substitutes have a similar or even greater environmental footprint? We'd rather believe that "this is the right thing and everyone should do it." On the flip side, if we decide that climate change is a scam, feeling certain saves us the effort of having to ask tough questions about our actions.

Feeling safe is the bait that most often appears when we consider conversations we *avoid having* because of how we think they might go. Sure, making a change in the world might require us to get other people on board. But think back to that list of perceived traits of a typical environmentalist, in chapter 3. Do we really want to risk someone calling us a crazy, self-righteous tree hugger (or whatever the equivalent is for advocates within your movement)? Remember that time you asked your boss, neighbor, parent, or team for something you cared about, and someone shut you down? It stings! It would be a lot safer to keep our concerns to ourselves and maybe enjoy the occasional gripe session with like-minded advocates.

One of the best ways to stay safe is to justify to yourself why taking action will never work. Too often we choose being right and righteous over taking effective action because it keeps us safe. But staying safe is a sucker's prize for not being effective.

Now, you may not recognize yourself in this image of the withdrawn activist, quietly being right in the corner. You may say, "I don't keep myself safe; I have no problem standing up and telling people what we need to change. I constantly get shot down, but I keep standing up." We've joked about it this way: "I would love to be a savior, but I will settle for being a martyr."

This is a fair description of us in our early stages of activism, like the MIT campaign described earlier. What we learned was that being a martyred activist, while it appeared courageous to some, was actually a way of keeping ourselves safe from investing the time and energy needed to solve problems.

The hidden nature of the bait creates the inauthenticity in this whole situation. We don't walk around telling people that our goal in life is to be right, righteous, certain, and safe. We tell everyone that we want a better world! The reality is that we want both. And nothing is wrong with wanting both. People are complicated. We run astray by pretending we are simple.

Exercise 11
Identify the bait in the trap

Consider the conversation you started reflecting on in chapter 3. How has your way of being, your background conversation, and your framing of the problem allowed you to be right, perhaps while making the other person wrong? How have you set yourself up to feel righteous? Are you taking the stance that you are certain about your ideas, actions, and strategies? Does your approach allow you to stay safe from confrontation, embarrassment, hard work, looking bad, getting in trouble, or other consequences?

Turn back to table 3, and look through the column of bait examples. Which baits resonate as hidden commitments that you were chasing, perhaps at the expense of being effective?

Map out your pitfall

Now that you have learned a little more about background conversations, being stuck, and bait, along with ways of being, let's take a moment to revisit your own situation.

Exercise 12
Map the pitfall

Consider the conversation that did not go the way you wanted it to go or that you have been avoiding.

Identify your background conversation. How are you perceiving the basic problem with the world? What do you find yourself saying about yourself and others?

Identify your way of being. What is your stance and tone when you address the problem? How do others feel and what do they think of you? What's it like for them being around you?

Identify the cost of being stuck. What are you giving up by being stuck? What is the cost of your not being effective? What goals and aspirations are you not achieving? What collateral damage are you creating?

Identify the bait in the trap. Have your framing of the problem and your way of being allowed you to be right? Righteous? Certain? Safe? What are you gaining, even when your conversation isn't working?

The very act of naming a pitfall may help you see a pathway out of it. We have seen this happen in our workshops. We'll hear a chuckle, and then a participant will say, "Well, I'm not going to use *that* strategy anymore!" This may well be your experience. If you realized that you have been staying safe by avoiding conversations, you may also feel some anxiety. This is because you have become aware that you now want to make a jump.

This may, however, not be your experience. Often, it takes a bit more courage to truly let go of the bait, a bit more energy to pull yourself out of the trap, and a bit more imagination and planning before you are ready to try something new.

In the next chapter, we offer a key to this next step: getting clear on what we really want and daring to share it with ourselves and others. When we can articulate something we want more than we want the bait, we can let it go.

chapter 4 summary

- We often persist with our ways of being and strategies even when we're not getting the results we want.

- We stay stuck because we still benefit from the status quo in subtle ways. Those benefits are the "bait" in a pitfall trap of our own making.

- The common pitfalls for advocates each have their own background conversation, cost of being stuck, and bait. These include "holier than thou," "someone should," "lone wolf," and "I know what progress is." We can't dig out of the pitfall until we let go of the bait.

- Bait usually involves getting to feel *right*, *righteous*, and *certain* about complicated issues. When we retreat to our group of fellow advocates, we get to stay *safe* from confrontation.

- *Do the work*: In looking at a specific conversation that has gotten stuck, identify your own pitfall, including your particular cost of being stuck and the bait. We all fall into pitfalls—we can laugh and poke fun at ourselves when we know we are all in this together. The key to getting out of pitfalls is taking responsibility for recognizing when you're stuck and for getting unstuck.

5

Dare to Share
Moving past the talking points

Why do we care enough about issues and problems in the world to dive into polarization and gridlock? Usually at the root of our advocacy is something that inspires us, such as our love for our family, community, or physical place in the world. That love and inspiration might extend more broadly to our country or to human and other life. We might draw inspiration from a dream or vision for how those things could be in the future. When it feels like our people, places, and dreams are under threat, we mobilize and advocate.

A funny thing happens, however, when conversations get stuck. In an argument or debate, sharing what we love can make us feel too vulnerable. We may also fear it wouldn't be effective if the other person doesn't share our priorities. Instead, we talk about what is wrong with the world in a more objective way. We describe problems and solutions in terms we think will persuade others. We focus on what is wrong with others, their behavior or ideas. We attach ourselves to the bait we described in chapter 4: getting to feel right, righteous, certain, and safe.

To shift the conversation, we can begin by reconnecting with ourselves and what matters most. Bringing that forward, along with a new way of being, creates a completely new context for conversation.

Here's a short story from Gabriel that we'll use as an example for this exploration:

> Our yogurt containers were number 5 plastic, and we couldn't recycle number 5. So for a while I'd pick them out of our blue bin and put them in a reusable grocery bag so I could deposit them in the "Gimme 5" container at Whole Foods. Several months went by and my wife, Sarah, hadn't caught on to the practice, so I reminded her that number 5 needed to go into the bag.
>
> The odds were in my favor. She shares my values around this, she loves me, and she knows I'm committed to making the world better and she married me for it. And yet that first conversation had zero effect. After a second, third, and fourth reminder, she started sorting out number 5, but she would only catch maybe one out of three number 5 containers. For a few more months I picked number 5 out of the bin, but each time I grew a little more resentful. Eventually, I asked her again, "Please put the number 5 in the bag."
>
> Then I got this look and I could tell we weren't on the same page. I thought maybe if she had my context, my education about the situation, my rationale, it would help. I started sharing my reasons for putting the right thing in the right bin:
>
> • It's the right thing to do.

- It's simple. You just need to find the number and if it says five, put it in the Whole Foods bag.
- If we put nonrecyclables in the recycling bin, it's called "contamination," and if there's too much contamination, the whole load might get dumped. Thus, putting the wrong thing in the bin not only threatens our recycling but threatens our entire neighborhood's recycling.

At this point, Sarah's look was shifting—but not in a good way. For the next few weeks, she quit sorting number 5 entirely. I think she even took a few containers out of my bag and tossed them in the blue bin for me to find. Finally, I came back with a system: "You put all the potentially recyclable things at the end of the kitchen counter, and each day I'll sort them into the appropriate place."

This seemed to be working. But after several months, Sarah said to me, "You know, I taught my parents how to recycle. I taught my grandparents how to recycle. And I taught my friends' parents to recycle. I used to love recycling. Now, living with you, I no longer want to recycle."

So here I am, months into this supposed solution, and the result is that my wife's upset, I seem to have depleted rather than supported her motivation to recycle, and we've allocated a considerable portion of our scarce counter space to my recycling sorting operation.

In reflecting on this situation, Gabriel could see that he was in a pitfall. He was attached to the bait of being right and righteous about recycling correctly. He suffered the costs of not moving forward on recycling and creating some collateral damage in the relationship. But seeing that was not quite enough to get him out of the trap.

Connect with internal motivations

To move forward, Gabriel had to confront another layer of inauthenticity. The reasons he gave Sarah for correctly recycling were not why he himself recycled nor why he wanted to share his commitment to recycling with her—they were reasons designed to sound right and righteous to persuade her. Getting honest with himself, he realized that he is indifferent about sorting recyclables correctly. He'd much prefer that there was a single bin and that either there was a single-stream system that didn't rely on his sorting at home or that everything was recyclable. What he really wants, what inspired him to recycle in the first place, is a beautiful world free of waste as we know it. In that world, people easily recycle, lovingly imitating nature's ingenious use of each creature's by-products.

And in fact, through the whole ongoing conflict over recycling, he was distracting himself from something he wanted even more—a certain quality of relationship with his wife, Sarah. When he set aside *being* a pretentious know-it-all jerk and took on *being* love and abundance, he saw that what he really wanted was to be "Sarah's partner on a journey, exploring together how we can best contribute to the world." Instead of sharing a vulnerable expression that touched his heart, he had gotten caught up in playing a smaller, safer game called "put the right thing in the right bin," something he could rationalize with impersonal facts.

We will come back to Gabriel's story and share the conclusion later in this chapter. For now, let us ask you, Why is your issue so important? Why should people vote? Why should people care about global warming? Why should you be concerned about human trafficking? Take a moment to reflect on your own issue of choice.

Exercise 13
Why is your endeavor important to you?

Choose a topic, issue, or cause that is important to you. Consider the list of issues from exercise 1 and the topic of the stuck conversation you identified in exercise 2.

In your notebook, at the top of a new page, write "[Insert your cause here] is important because . . ."

Then, underneath that prompt, complete the sentence several (as many as ten) times with whichever responses first come to you.

Be sure to write down all the reasons and rationales that you have given to other people when explaining why they should care and act on that issue.

Notice if your list includes some of the patterns we have noticed in ourselves and among our workshop participants:

- We frame causes as being about abstract issues and problems that are not about our experiences, values, or feelings.

- We translate our personal values, aspirations, and dreams into "external motivations," like danger and dollars. We communicate those external motivations—the costs and benefits of taking a particular course of action—and we withhold what originally inspired us.

- We do the above because we are told that other people don't value what we value.

Notice if, in this context, you have had the following experience:

- By not sharing ourselves, our heart, and our love, by only sharing "facts," we avoid the risk of being judged. We hold onto the bait of being safe and avoid being vulnerable.

- We try to engage other people, but they don't re-create for themselves the inspired, internally driven experience we say we want to share. In the process, our own internally driven experience slips away from us.

- We grow frustrated and resigned and rely even more heavily on external justification and motivation for both ourselves and others.

The core inauthenticity is that I care, I love, I have a vision of the future I want, but these aren't the focus of my advocacy. My heart is moved by something, but that's not what I'm sharing. What's more, even though I won't share it with you, I am upset that what moves me doesn't move you.

How do we break this cycle? How do we share what really matters to us?

We can start by applying what we call "the football test" to our motivations, reasons, and justifications. As activists, we sometimes wonder why it is so much easier to mobilize millions of people behind a football game than behind a social cause. But in a way, the answer is simple. If you were to ask people on the street headed to a football game, "Why are you going to the game?" they'd probably say something like

- "Because it's awesome!"
- "My team rocks!"
- "I love going!"
- "I'm a big fan."

If you pushed them and asked, "Why?" they might struggle to articulate some facts or reasons why it's awesome, why they love it, or why their team rocks. But they'd probably lean back on their most basic answer, "Because I love it."

"Because I love it" or "I'm a fan" are examples of internal or self-determined motivations. They are not dependent on any outside circumstance or rationale. They are expressions of one's interest or one's self or an end in and of itself. No rationale or justification is required for why I love football. I just do. The football test is this: can you boil down the issue you care about into this kind of simple, self-evident statement?

For example, Jason describes his motivation for tackling climate change this way:

> I am in awe of snowy mountains and I love coastal cities. I want to make sure those places are around for my children and grandchildren to enjoy. I love getting my brain working on complex problems. I am inspired working together with other people who share dreams for a better world.

Now reflect for a moment on how we share what's most important to us, including the reasons you created in exercise 13. Are any of those reasons self-determined? Do they point toward outside circumstances or rely on shared cultural values to justify the importance? Consider this example: Ending human trafficking is important to me because

- "People are suffering."
- "There are more than half a million victims each year."
- "It's the right thing to do."
- "Children should not be bought and sold."

These are all important and valid reasons why we should take action to end human trafficking. They aren't bad or wrong. However, like Gabriel's reasons for recycling correctly, these don't share our internal (or self-determined) motivations.

You may be thinking, "Hold on. Ending human trafficking [or substitute your cause here] is of personal importance to me and I am consciously valuing it." "I personally value having the right material in the right bin." "I'm internally motivated by [my cause]." If that's true, we're going to help you embody and express that motivation in your communication. That way you can benefit from the experience of internal motivation yourself and might possibly make it available to others. This shift can begin with our language.

Reflecting back on Gabriel's recycling story, he was sharing external motivations. Instead of sharing something he loved, he tried to shame his wife into recycling correctly with facts and rationale. We all have a tendency to experience our own internal motivations while projecting external motivations onto others.[1] Not only does this fall short of sharing internal motivations, but external motivations have a tendency to displace or crowd out internal motivations. In the process, both Gabriel's and his wife's internal motivations for recycling became diminished.

If you are already clear about your internal motivations and you are comfortable sharing them in potentially polarized conversations, that is great. However, you may still find yourself getting stuck when other people just don't seem to care. If so, then the work for you may be in listening and drawing out the *other person's* internal motivations and embracing the tension between your motivations in a productive way. We support that work in chapter 7, but your work with a buddy in this chapter will help you prepare. It is also worth carefully reflecting on whether that internal motivation is the only motivation for how you are showing up or you also have a commitment to being right, righteous, or certain that may be interfering with your message. That is the work of chapters 4 and 6.

We are guessing, however, that the majority of responses you wrote in exercise 13 refer to external circumstances like Gabriel's justifications for recycling correctly. These include problems, symptoms, and consequences; cultural valuations of right and wrong; and other facts, reasons, and justifications that are external to you. And you may have a tendency to hide from yourself how externally justified your motivations are.

You, like us, want to live a self-determined life. For example, Gabriel would prefer to think "it's the right thing to do" is an internally motivated expression. However, it references a shared notion of what's right; it's not his personal expression of what he loves. The expression is insufficient for sharing his internally motivated experience with others. It's possible that underneath the expression is a self-determined motivation. However, when you share "do the right thing" with people who are doing the wrong thing, how do you think that will get heard? Will they be internally lit up and inspired, or are they going to experience guilt, shame, or a social pressure to change?

Apply the football test. If you asked truly passionate football fans why football is important to them, can you imagine them responding "because it's the right thing to do"? Can you imagine them using responses that are analogous to what you listed in exercise 13?

Jason's inspiration for working on climate change that we shared earlier did not come from a statement that began with "I work on climate change because." Instead, climate change is a *context*, inside which he gets to make a contribution and do what he loves.

Here's another test. Do you experience an inner pressure to behave in accord with what's right? For yourself or others in your crowd, can advocating for your cause be challenging, tiring, or frustrating, even to the point of being psychologically exhausting or causing burnout? Can it create tension in your relationships or prevent you from fully sharing yourself with others? Do you avoid certain people entirely? These descriptions are all consistent with experiencing motivations that are not internal. The need to continually justify your cause to yourself and others is tiring; it zaps vitality. It's not self-determined.

Now take a moment to see if you can classify the motivations you articulated in exercise 13.

Exercise 14
Notice what motivations you're sharing or not sharing

Review each response you created in exercise 13, and label it with the appropriate type of motivation, *self-determined* or *external*.

- Self-determined or internal motivations are self-referential—for example, "I sing to sing." Or they point back to you—for example, "I sing because I love to sing," "I work to create peace in the world to create peace in the world," "I do it for the fun of it," "I do it for the challenge," "It fulfills me," "It's what I love," "It's who I am."

- External motivations point to something outside you—for example, "It's the right thing to do (according to a moral

Continued on next page

authority or my facts that I can share with you)," "The status quo is wrong, dangerous, costly, unjust, inefficient, illegal, or bad for our health," "It's good/bad for business, the environment, or society."

Assess only the language you wrote, considering how someone else would experience the communication. Do not take into consideration your expanded thoughts behind what is written.

Notice the mix of motivations you shared. Notice which you shared first and which you shared only after several others.

Notice any tendency to want to score your responses as being more self-determined than they actually are. Notice if you want to add more responses or tweak your existing responses, perhaps to "cheat" on your own assessment.

Consider if other motivations came to mind when you first did the exercise that you left out entirely—you decided, for whatever reason, not to write them down, not to share them. Maybe now you're tempted to add them to your original list. Maybe you're even more tempted to keep them out. Write them down separately.

Share your reflections with a buddy, and invite their perspective on what feels the most authentic to them and what inspires them.

Consider that the reason we find it so challenging to get others to internalize what's important to us is that we haven't internalized what's important to us. In fact, we tend toward the opposite. We fall in love with something—an idea, a place, a person, a group of people—but instead of sharing our heart, sharing our internal motivation, we translate our internal motivations into external motivations that we believe will speak to others. Or we borrow other people's external motivations to justify what we love.

You may have already noticed that simply changing your rationale may not seem to cut it. "I love to put the right thing in the right bin because I love to put the right thing in the right bin" could sound a bit silly. It might not sound authentic to you. Although it could, and that may be a much more pleasant way to experience your personal recycling practice. Try it out.

If putting the right thing in the right bin (or whatever your cause is) doesn't involve a sense of purpose or satisfaction in and of itself, it may not be what you want most.

At this point, you may think, "It doesn't matter whether my motivation or theirs is internal or not. We need to save the planet or we'll all be dead" or "Basic human rights are too important an issue for us to waste time with how people feel about it." In this case, the *power and influence strategies* we mentioned in chapter 1 may work for you, and you should try them. However, you may be in a situation (like Gabriel's marriage) where the other person's flourishing really matters to you. You may need to build long-term, sustained engagement with the person to achieve your goals. In that context, communicating external motivations (as Gabriel did) may inadvertently turn the person away from the behaviors and values you are seeking to inspire. They may sacrifice the quality of your relationship and even, eventually, contribute to your own burnout.

In fact, many research studies in positive psychology and organization studies suggest that internal motivations support behaviors and outcomes that are keys to success. These include creativity, persistence in the face of challenging tasks, psychological well-being, cognitive flexibility and deep learning, work involving complexity, positive emotions, and engagement.[2] Internal motivations correlate with inner peace, deep acceptance of oneself and others, trust, and practical behavior.

In highly effective companies built around a social or environmental mission, employees are more likely to be experiencing internal motivations. These correlate with their experience of meaning and purpose; a sense of fulfillment, accomplishment, or satisfaction; positive relationships; and engagement. External motivations like "it's the right thing to do" are insufficient for creating those outcomes.

Express what you really want

Consider for a moment that your cause, the issue you have been saying is really important to you, doesn't really begin to express what you really want. At best it's merely one small piece inside a much larger possibility or idea for the world. That larger possibility, that dream, is an internal expression—an expression of your heart and an expression of who you are for the world. If that possibility were widely shared, the issue you're now focused on might get resolved as a side effect or spillover benefit.

Whatever future you really want, it will ring true to your heart as a purpose worth pursuing in and of itself.

"I want inspired and purposeful people because that is what I want." No secondary reason is necessary. "I want a loving partnership with my wife." "I want whole people and whole families." When you can articulate the greater possible future for yourself, you'll be able to experience your internal motivation for yourself and share it with others. It will move you. You may tear up just thinking about it.

Exercise 15
Envision what you really want

Consider that the topic, issue, or cause you chose in exercise 13 doesn't begin to express what you really want.

Consider that, perhaps, what you previously identified is something you're indifferent about or maybe at most one small possible expression of what you'd really love to see expressed in the world.

Begin to consider what possibility, vision, or dream makes your heart light up. What do you really love?

What would you really like to share with the world?

What might be worth working toward even if it were a thousand-year ambition, for which you would never see the result?

What would be worth working toward as your own self-expression, regardless of the result?

Play with completing these sentence prompts and see what lights you up:

- I have a dream where . . .
- What I'm committed to creating is . . .
- What I'm standing for is . . .

Continued on next page

Finally, don't be limited by the prompts. Craft your own aspirations in ways that speak to you.

Work with your buddy to share your answers to these prompts with each other. Practice listening to and coaching your buddy so you understand each other's answers. This paired work will be invaluable preparation as you engage in other, more challenging conversations.

Once you've landed on what really inspires you, share it. Give other people the opportunity to be inspired by what you are up to and the choice to contribute (or not). Give them the opportunity simply to be inspired about your being inspired. You'll be surprised who may love to "play football" [insert your dream here] with you— perhaps someone who you never could have believed would play with you.

Being able to declare *what* you really want is one aspect of daring to share. The other aspect is *how* you show up as you declare it. What is your way of being? In chapter 3 we helped you "know what you bring." Now you get to determine what you want to bring. Let go of the bait. Let go of your old way of being. Focus your attention on what you really want to create. What becomes available to you as a way of being?

Otto Scharmer, a leadership scholar and lecturer at MIT, describes an experience of "presence." It is a special quality of attention and listening. It arises when we set aside our background conversation and quiet our minds. We bring an open mind, open heart, and open will to the conversation. He describes "presencing" as the ability to release the habits of the past and participate in an emerging new future.[3] This can be that moment for you.

Exercise 16
Create a new way of being

Consider the stuck conversation you have been reflecting on for the past few chapters. Imagine saying the following:

> Going forward in this conversation and relationship, you can count on me to be _____, which is consistent with the future I really want.

How would you fill in the blank? Try to be as succinct as possible—a single adjective or a short phrase that you can say to yourself and awaken that sensibility.

This is a critical moment in the book. Much of the work we have done so far is to make room for you to create a new way of being, one that could possibly generate new approaches, new actions, and new results.

We can't tell you what to write here. This is a moment of transformation, and the power to create is up to you. We can simply pose some questions for you to consider:

- What is the future that you really want for your relationship and for the world?
- What way of being would be consistent with that future?
- If you were in that future right now, how would you feel—what would be your way of being?

These can be very hard questions to address intellectually. We have found that people get more clarity through an experiential

Continued on next page

exercise. We offer the guided meditation below as a way to help you get in touch with the future you want.[4] If you just rolled your eyes, you are not alone. In our workshops, it takes a moment to get people settled into this practice. Then we often hear—even from hard-minded, skeptical business executives—that it was the most valuable piece of our work together.

Exercise 17
Guided meditation

Sit upright and comfortably, take a deep breath, and slowly read the following, letting yourself experience it piece by piece:

> It's thirty years from now, and there are still problems in the world. But things have come a long way. In fact, you are surprised and impressed by how far things have come. Some people still struggle, but overall, people are more healthy and prosperous than you could have imagined. Structures are in place to support those who would like support. There has been a positive shift in the health of planet Earth. The skies and waters are cleaner. Species and habitats are recovering. Nations are more peaceful than you imagined could be possible. More people than you ever imagined are inspired and alive, contributing to making the world better together.

Close your eyes and visualize this.

Now, continue:

As you inhabit this place and time, know that you had something to do with it. It wasn't you by yourself, and perhaps nothing you did singly was as ambitious as you thought you might do when you were young. But nevertheless, what you did accomplish—working inside this symphony of what everyone accomplished—was enough. And now you are standing in this place. While there are still problems to be solved, it is clear that we are going to get there from here. Nothing is insurmountable. The world is in the midst of becoming something very special that you are excited to pass on to generations to come.

Let yourself experience the following aspects of that future:

What's in the news?

What do we get to eat?

How do people spend their time?

Consider that people you never thought would be allies have contributed together to create this profound shift. What does this look like?

How do they get to be with one another?

How do you get to be?

Now take a moment to close your eyes and visualize this future more concretely, and experience that way of being—how it feels to you, how it occurs to other people.

When you are ready, turn to a blank page in a journal or notebook, and take ten minutes to do some free writing—whatever comes to your mind. Include any reflections on what you saw, how it felt, and particularly your way of being.

In our workshops, when we ask people to do this meditation and to create new ways of being, we ask them to say their ways of being out loud. We type them onto a slide so that everyone can see. Then after the workshops, we collect those words from the slides as data. Figure 3 shows what we have heard.

Figure 3 New ways of being created by our workshop participants[5]

Be inspired by this picture, latch onto a word that captures your imagination, and make it your own. The point is, there is no right way of being. Try them out. Find one that inspires you and is appropriate to your situation and what you want to accomplish. Create a way of being that's authentically aligned with the future you want.

Alice, from chapter 3, noticed that she was being righteous and judgmental in reaction to her mother's righteousness and judgment about gay people. When she let go of this way of being, she saw that the world she wanted was one filled with compassion and love. She could be compassionate and loving and create the world she wanted now, starting with her mother.

Once you've identified a possible new way of being that excites you, that is authentic to who you want to be and the future you want to create, consider the conversation you have been reflecting on through chapters 3 and 4. Put yourself in the other person's shoes for a moment. Take on that person's experience of the world. Ask yourself, would this way of being make a difference for me? Would it engage and inspire me to see you take this on? This kind of empathic inquiry is very important. It gets at what Scharmer calls "open heart."[6]

Gabriel saw he wanted a partnership with Sarah where they were exploring how to best contribute to the world together. His fixation on the number 5 plastic recycling was destroying something he cared much more about.

> When Sarah said to me, "I used to love recycling. Now, living with you, I no longer want to recycle," it left me speechless.
>
> That day I took on reflecting on how this had come to be. I got clear on what I really wanted and the way of being I wanted to bring to our interaction. I said the following: "In relation to number 5 in the recycling, I have been a condescending, know-it-all jerk. While I was saying I want the right thing in the right bin, really I wanted to be right and make you wrong and perhaps shame you into recycling correctly. I recognize I diminished you and the quality of our relationship and I am sorry. In the future you can count on me to be *loving*. What I really want is a profound partnership where we're exploring how we can best contribute to the world together."

She was shocked, inspired, and hesitant. I could tell she wanted to believe me, she was moved by what I said, and she was skeptical. That didn't matter. I was committed. I abandoned the sorting pile and for the next few weeks, I pulled number 5 out of the recycling bin and put it in the Whole Foods bag. I had the feeling she was still putting number 5 in the recycling bin just to test me, yet each number 5 container in the blue bin was an opportunity to be loving. I kept on being loving and eventually the number 5 quit showing up in the wrong bin. But that wasn't the real win. The real win was who I got to be for my wife, and today it's who I get to be in front of my daughters.

Before moving forward, we want you to think deeply about this opportunity to create a new way of being in a conversation that matters to you, where you have a goal for improving the world in some way, however small or big.

Embody your new way of being

Once you write down a word or short phrase that captures your new way of being, really dwell in that way of being. Don't just say, "I will be more understanding now" or "I'll try to be more courageous." Let understanding or courage arise in your body. Feel it in your heart and in your mind. Let that feeling flow into how you see, how you listen, and what you say to yourself.

Your response at this moment may be "But I don't know how." That's actually fantastic. It's a sign that you are genuinely creating a way of being that is new for you.

Some Christians wear a bracelet engraved with the letters "WWJD" for "What would Jesus do?" A useful technique for anyone is to imagine someone in your life, or in your favorite story, who already exemplifies the way of being you want to create. Imagine that role model with your new way of being in your situation. How would they see the scene? How would they listen? What would they be saying to themselves, and to the other person? Inside that new way of being, what occurs to you to think, say, and do?

Reflect back on the conversation you explored in chapters 3 and 4. If you were to take on this new way of being, what would you find yourself saying about the conversation and situation?

One possible outcome is a shift in perspective. How does your sense of the problem shift? Inside that new way of being, what would you really like to make available in the world? Gabriel's objective changed from "the right thing in the right bin" to "a profound partnership where we're exploring how we can best contribute to the world together." A beautiful coemergence is possible as you go back and forth between creating a way of being and articulating a vision of what you want. The two are interrelated. Standing in a new way of being allows you to see a new possible future. Seeing a new possible future allows you to envision more possible ways of being that are consistent with that future.

Take a moment for another iteration of envisioning the future you want for the world and how you would be in it.

Another possible outcome is that your problem simply disappears. In Jason's MIT example from chapter 4, the new way of being "helpful" brought a shift in focus from the problem called "The administration isn't taking enough action" to the question "How could I support fellow students?"

You may find that your whole perspective on problems can shift. A problem-solving orientation often focuses on the immediate barriers we face and has us fixated on a limited set of possible reactions to the past and present. From your new way of being, you may step back from the problem, focus on the future you want to create, and start working backward from there. That perspective makes available a much larger space of possibilities for you and others to contribute toward the future you want.

- -

Exercise 18
Reframe the problem

Take a moment to deeply consider the new way of being that you have created and articulated in the previous exercises. Visualize yourself being that way in the conversation that has gotten stuck.

From this new perspective, this new vantage point, write down what you really want to have happen in the conversation—an outcome or future quality of the relationship that would make you feel like you had manifested the future you envision.

Now write down what you observe about the current state of the situation. What is the gap between the current state and what you want? This may include your own behaviors, thoughts, and feelings. It may include the other person's behaviors, thoughts, and feelings as you understand them.

What new actions could you take?

What new conversations could you have?

Often when people get to this point in the inquiry, they start to notice a tricky issue. You may find that you have articulated what you want and a new way of being. You have recognized how your old way of being and bait have gotten in your way. You are feeling a shift inside yourself. But you may anticipate that the other person won't be ready to hear all of this from you. They may continue to expect and respond to your old way of being. That brings us to the next step in our journey.

chapter 5 summary

- It takes courage to let go of the bait. The key is getting clear on what we really want and daring to share that with others.

- Often at the root of our advocacy is something that inspires us—our love for people, our love of life, and an idea of how the world could be. Because it feels too vulnerable to share that, we talk about what is wrong with the world in a more objective way.

- Mapping out our motivations can be helpful in understanding why an issue or line of advocacy is important to us. Some of these motivations are more self-determined and internal; others are more externally driven reasons or forms of psychological pressure.

- To get a conversation unstuck, we first have to reconnect with ourselves and what matters most. Bringing that forward can create a completely new basis for conversation.

- One way to get in touch with our internal motivations is to visualize and let ourselves dwell in the future we want to create. That experience can help us see what matters to us. It can also help us experience a new way of being.

- Creating and taking on a new way of being can shift the way we see the problems in front of us and the conversations where we have gotten stuck.

- *Do the work*: Identify the deeper, heartfelt motivations for why your issue or line of advocacy is important to you. Use the reflection and visualization exercises in this chapter to get in touch with the future you want to create and a new way of being that is aligned with that future.

6

Start Talking
Bringing conversations back to life

If you've been doing the work with us up to now, you have accomplished the following:

- You have identified at least one conversation toward improving the world that did not go the way you wanted it to go. You may have identified a conversation that you want to have but have been putting off or avoiding. In either situation, you have identified a real conversation that matters to you that is stuck.

- You have reflected on your way of being in that situation and how it is tied up with your conversation with yourself: your view of yourself and the other person, the things you are thinking and feeling but not necessarily saying.

- You have identified the bait and the costs of being stuck.

- At some point during this process of self-reflection, you've found yourself squirming, blushing, or chuckling to yourself. You've caught a glimpse of how your way of being and speaking is out of alignment with the complexity of who you are in the present and with the future you want to create.

- You have gotten clearer on what you really want in the situation, and you have created a new way of being that may be more authentic and effective in light of those goals.

If you have done all the exercises to this point, you have made real progress and begun changing your side of the conversation. Now the question is, How do we take action to make a difference?

The first thing to acknowledge is that moving from a journey of self-reflection to a new actual conversation can provoke some real doubts and concerns. Very often we will see people read aloud their description of their pitfall and acknowledge this: "I see how this may not be working, and I see this new way of being I want to embody, *but* . . ." What comes after the "but" is some description of the situation that is centered on the past. Often it focuses on how the other person in the conversation has been thinking, feeling, or being.

- "I just don't think I can get through to that person."
- "It's too late; I have soured the relationship and missed the opportunity."
- "We're both being self-righteous in the situation; I might be able to give up that way of being, but I don't think he's going to."

Do we want you to figure out what pitfall the other person is in and name it so the reflection can be balanced and fair? Sadly, no. After all the work we've done on self-reflection, it would be great if we could hold up a mirror and force others to be self-reflective, to take responsibility for their part of the conversation!

In fact, this is a huge trap. You can't make anyone else be self-reflective. The only reason you got this far is because you chose to pick up this book, you chose to do the exercises, you chose to reflect and learn. All we've done is give you the tools and let you know that we're in this together. If you try to point out someone else's way of being, the bait you think that person has grabbed onto, and the consequences of being stuck, two results are almost certain: first, you won't see the whole picture because you don't really know what's going on inside the person's head, and second, you will likely provoke defensiveness and entrenchment.

This whole inquiry involves getting vulnerable, exposing what we don't usually expose, letting go of past known behavior, and exploring possible futures that are unfamiliar to us. So you'll notice a tendency to protect yourself and the emergence of new pitfalls. For instance, identifying other people's pitfalls is a great way to make yourself right, righteous, and certain! And it's a great way to keep yourself safe from having to take on making a difference.

So what can we do?

It's time for another thought experiment—an imaginary conversation in which you acknowledge your pitfall and its consequences out loud to the other person.

Exercise 19
Build a new conversation

Imagine a new conversation with the other person where you have previously been stuck. Fill in the blanks with your pitfall diagnosis, and imagine making this statement out loud to the other person. You may want to change the phrasing so that it feels more natural to you, but make sure you include each of the elements.

I want to talk with you about _____ (prior conversation or avoided conversation). I have come to see that up to this point I have been _____ (old ways of being), which is not consistent with my values and who I aspire to be.

While I've been saying I want _____ (stated goals for a better future), really I was also going for _____ (bait).

I see some unfortunate consequences of this approach, which include _____ (consequences of being stuck).

I am sorry to have taken this approach. I want to create a new way to engage.

Going forward you can count on me to be _____ (new way of being), which is consistent with the future I really want. And I want you to call me on it if you catch me slipping back into old habits.

Depending on your situation, having this conversation may feel like jumping off a cliff. It may feel awkward to disclose so much of your inner landscape. That's great! Letting go of the bait and moving beyond staying safe should make you feel vulnerable.

Remember that this is a thought experiment—it is not always the case that you should literally say this aloud to the other person. Even just envisioning saying it, and role-playing with a buddy, can help push you over a mental hump. Beneath all the anxiety about coming clean, people often experience another feeling: spaciousness, freedom, a sense of possibility.

You may notice, however, that Gabriel did follow the exercise 19 template when changing the conversation with Sarah in chapter 5. It was a pivot point in their interaction around the recycling bin. When does it make sense to say words like these out loud with the other person?

The power of apology

Our script in exercise 19 is basically an apology. If done well, an apology can transform and strengthen a relationship. It can generate a willingness to cooperate going forward. It can be a demarcation point, breaking existing behavior patterns, and it can offer a commitment to cocreate a more desirable future starting now.

The trick is that apologies need to be wholehearted to be effective. John Kador's book *Effective Apology* is a great resource and lines up well with research by Stanford social psychologist Karina Schumann.[1] Table 4 is based on Kador's and Schumann's work.

Table 4 Elements of wholehearted and effective apologies

Wholehearted apology (effective)	Halfhearted apology (ineffective)	Nonapology (harmful)
Specify the offense, acknowledge the harm, and concede the facts.	Hint at the offense, downplay the impact, or debate the facts.	Justify or defend one's behavior; dispute the impact or the facts.
Make a full admission of wrongdoing, accepting responsibility without blaming circumstances.	Provide excuses; share responsibility or blame with the other party (or a third party).	Sidestep responsibility.
Explicitly express remorse (e.g. use the words "I am sorry").	Posture remorse (e.g., say, "I'm sorry you interpreted . . .").	Withhold remorse.
Inquire into and offer what is required to repair the damage.	Make a contingent offer, or offer words without action.	Question the motives of the apology seeker.
Make a new commitment for the future, including a pledge to not repeat the offending conduct.	Offer a commitment contingent on the other party or external circumstances. Suggest the possibility of repeating the offending conduct.	Commit to repeat the offending conduct.

Our experience is that by envisioning who you want to be (as we did in chapter 5), you're more likely to generously express each of the five effective elements and create a powerful apology.

You may find yourself reacting to the language "I am sorry." As one of our students put it,

I think in some cases to say "I'm sorry" is disempowering—
it takes away from your message and puts you on the
back foot. . . . I would tend toward language like "I can
understand / recognize how my actions / words would
have occurred as X."

Here is why we have found taking responsibility in the language of an apology to be an important part of the process. While at first glance "I am sorry" seems to give away our power, putting us on the "back foot," the alternative puts the onus on the other person to change. Although you might say, "I can understand how *you* would interpret my actions as X," the background conversation here is "But you're wrong, and here is how you should interpret me correctly!" You may appear to stand firm, but this approach actually gives your power away. It makes your progress in the conversation dependent on their shifting their interpretation. A genuine "sorry" does something different: it frees you up to try a new approach. It frames what's not working as independent of them or other forces external to you. That gives you power.

Research shows that partial, safe, or sympathetic apologies, like our student suggests above, don't work.[2] Or worse, they can backfire. Full apologies that accept responsibility are more likely to be effective. Even when legal benefits are not at stake, there is a real psychological benefit to withholding the words "I'm sorry."[3] Thus, to make a full apology, to say "I'm sorry," is to let go of psychological bait.

This expression of vulnerability creates a different kind of power *with* the other person. It sidesteps the mutual attempts to have power over each other's thoughts and actions. A powerful apology

- exercises your own autonomy, overcoming short-term psychological gain in pursuit of your own deeper values
- models that possibility for everyone who witnesses it
- validates the perceptions of the other party, which can leave them feeling whole and available to focus on their own deeper values and commitments
- frees both of you up to play together, creating new solutions and pathways that transcend the circumstances that previously appeared to be stuck

Table 5 includes a few examples from our workshops where participants admit to creating pitfalls:

Table 5 Examples of people's acknowledgments of the pitfalls they have created

Addressing avoided conversations	Addressing conversations that didn't go well
To my uncle Vicente: In relation to your business in the oil production world, my way of being has been to stay safe by not bringing it up. While I've been saying I want you to stop partaking in this unsustainable industry, really I've also been hoping to be right and call you out on it. The consequences of my approach have been creating distance, diminishing you and our relationship.	In a conversation with my employee Natalie about Styrofoam cups, my way of being has been pious and know-it-all. While I've been saying I want a win-win solution, really I was also trying to be right and recognized as the expert. The consequence has been a lack of trust all around. I am sorry for my past approach.
To a board member of my organization: In relation to our canceling our recycling service, my way of being has been timid. While I've been saying I want to find more impactful ways of saving money, really I've also been trying to avoid conflict. The result is that I am missing an opportunity to contribute to the organization by creating alignment with our core company values and my own vision for the future.	To food service executives about preventing human rights abuses in your supply chains: In our conversations, my way of being has been condescending and one sided. While I've been saying I want to prevent human trafficking and forced labor, really I have also been trying to feel like I made a difference by changing you. The consequences are that I have prevented us from connecting and created mutual frustration. I would like to take a new approach.

We have also seen this approach of "coming clean" work in a mix of conversation and writing. Laura Yates encountered our work as part of the Byron Fellowship.[4] She recounted the story of her senior trip, which we mention briefly in our preface.

We were less than a week away from graduating from college, and celebrating the past four years together, when the conversation moved to the topic of climate change. One of my closest friends said he thought scientists were just trying to scare everyone into changing their behavior. I snapped and yelled at him for not believing in science. I refused to listen to anything he had to say. I ended the conversation abruptly by saying "This is bullshit. I don't want to talk about this with you at all."

Everyone froze and got really quiet. The rest of the trip was really uncomfortable. In that moment, I shut down my ability to relate to my friends and completely lost the opportunity to have a valuable conversation about climate change.

With some coaching on pitfalls, I understood what I lost through my way of being in that conversation. I also realized I had the power to change the way both my friend and I remember the conversation. I could open it back up with a different way of being. So I wrote him this letter:

Nick, I wanted to talk to you and apologize for the way I acted on vacation. When you said you didn't believe in man-made climate change, I yelled at you and ended the conversation abruptly. By reacting this way, I wasn't being open-minded or a true friend—I was acting in an aggressive, dismissive manner that isn't characteristic of the type of friend or person I want to be.

I want to acknowledge now—because I didn't when we first had this conversation—that there is uncertainty in climate science. Uncertainty is inherent in all science.

The uncertainty scares me because it threatens the choices I've made in my life so far. Instead of being authentic and acknowledging the uncertainty, I purposefully diminished the value of what you were saying, asserting that I was right and you were wrong.

The way I reacted hurt our relationship and made everyone around us feel uncomfortable and distanced at a time when we should have been relaxing and enjoying our last few days together.

If I'd been speaking from a place of friendship and love, what I should have said is this: "There is some uncertainty about climate change science. Uncertainty is inherent in the scientific process. I hope that the predictions about man-made climate change aren't as bad as people say. However, I do think it's important for us as humans to understand the impact we have and take counter-measures in case we are causing these changes in the natural environment, which is why I've chosen to work and study in this field."

I hope you feel comfortable telling me and holding me accountable if I flip out like that again—whether it's at you or any of our friends. I know it seems strange for me to bring this up almost a month after it happened, but that exchange was one of the last ones we had before graduation, and I didn't want it to be a lasting memory. I want to let you know I really value our friendship and I sincerely apologize for acting in a way that didn't show you how much your friendship means to me.

Love,
Laura

When we read this letter, we were struck by the writer's vulnerability—admitting to uncertainty about climate change and apologizing are never easy. At the same time, we can hear the authenticity—the genuine desire to connect and relate to Nick. We can also see that Laura reasserts her values: why she has chosen to work and study in the field of environmental leadership. We were intensely curious to know the outcome.

> Once I finished writing this letter, I decided to call Nick and share it with him in the hopes that my reopening the conversation in a more positive way might help us strengthen our friendship. Reading Nick this letter forced me to be vulnerable and to open myself up to him, helping him feel more comfortable and willing to interact. After hearing me read the letter, Nick was quick to tell me he felt some guilt about the way he was being during our original conversation. He expressed an interest in learning more about climate change because it was something I was passionate about. He joked that we're both pretty passionate people, and it wasn't surprising to him that we'd gotten in an argument in the first place. Hearing him say that made me realize how much more powerful and effective I could be if I approached every conversation with the same amount of passion and a more thoughtful way of being.
>
> Through the difficult and awkward process of writing this letter, I got clear on why the (un)certainty around climate change science was such a hot-button issue for me. It's surprising and almost scary how many different layers I needed to pull back to get rid of the projections

of blame on Nick for how the conversation went and to find my own power in the situation.

Since this conversation took place, in conversations with my uncle, grandparents, coworkers, professors, and others, I've made a conscious effort to engage them with compassion and understanding as my ways of being. Conversations that I previously would have avoided have since become so productive!

It is one thing to declare a way of being that is aligned with the future you want to create. It is another matter entirely to create space for it and act on it. Creating space for a new way of being involves owning up to the history of the conversation first.

Exercise 20
Write a letter

Write a letter to the person with whom you have a stuck conversation. In the letter, acknowledge the different aspects of the pitfall. Use the previous "imaginary conversation" (exercise 19) and Laura's letter as inspiration, but use your own words—make it yours.

Note that as you draft the letter, you may find yourself at a loss for words after laying out the elements of the pitfall. You may think, "If my new way of being is about understanding and openness, then it's not about what I am going to say. It is about how I am going to listen and the questions I am going to ask." This is fine, and in the next chapter we will address how to ask good questions. For now, you can start imagining what you'd like to ask the person—for example, "What has this conversation been like for you?"

Now imagine using the letter to engage the person. You may prefer to send the letter or to read it to the person aloud. Or, you may use it as a way to organize your thoughts before a new conversation.

You will encounter a variety of responses

When you imagine naming the pitfall and owning up to your past approach, what do you imagine happening? What thoughts run through your head? What does it feel like in your body? What do you imagine your conversation partner feeling? What could you imagine your partner thinking and then saying?

If you go through with using the letter, there is a real possibility that the person will be moved and inspired. They may share their own candid reflections on their way of being. Together you will articulate and explore a common ground that you didn't know could exist. You could get creative about solutions to problems that had seemed insurmountable. Or, as in Gabriel's situation, you may abandon your old problems entirely for the pursuit of something greater.

Of course, this may not happen right away. A second scenario is that the person will be intrigued by your new approach but suspicious. One of our students reported that he took a new approach to his wife's driving style, which he saw as too fast and dangerous. He had been either arguing or avoiding riding with her. From a new way of being, he tried appreciating her driving skills and sharing his fear of high speeds. Her initial reaction was "Something sounds fishy." When he stayed with the approach, she interrogated further: "What is going on with you?"

A response like this is natural. Our colleagues, friends, and relatives have an expectation of how we are going to be. When we show up with a new way of being, we shouldn't expect them to be completely accepting. In the end, our student shared more of the full context of the pitfalls-and-pathways exercises he had been doing. He shared his hopes about the flourishing of his family and society. His wife heard where he was coming from and adjusted her driving style—staying closer to the speed limit and keeping pace with traffic.

Results require action, and action requires commitment

So far we have moved from letting go of an old way of being, with its associated trap and bait, to creating a new way of being. We have begun to envision new actions— writing a letter and having a new conversation.

What is the likelihood that you will take action, transform or create new conversations, and produce new results in the world now that you have a vision? That depends. What is your success rate for New Year's resolutions? Ours is awful. An important missing link between visions and resolutions on the one hand and actual actions on the other is *commitment*. And what we mean by "commitment" is not merely an idea in your head. It's a conversation in the world, a promise made to someone else.

Commitments that lead to action have a solid relationship to reality—both in time and in space. They are specific. If you want to have a new conversation, *exactly when and where are you going to have it*? An answer to "when" does not count if it's "someday" or "soon" or "eventually." Even "tomorrow" is problematic. We are always starting a new exercise regimen "tomorrow." Consider the difference between "Next week I am starting a new workout regimen" and "Next Tuesday at 7:00 a.m. I am starting a new workout regimen."

Exercise 21
Conversation commitment

Exactly when and where are you going to have the new conversation that embodies your new way of being where you had previously been stuck?

Now is a great time. If not now, when? Write down the time in your calendar or diary, or create an alarm or reminder in your phone—whatever system you reliably use.

If you need to schedule time with the person, text, call, or e-mail the person *right now* to set it up.

Ask someone to make you accountable. Share your letter or an outline of your conversation with your buddy, spouse, partner, colleague, or friend. Let the person know the exact time you'll be having your conversation and schedule a time with them to follow up and share what happens.

This is the chance to complete the work you have been doing in chapters 3 to 6.

If you haven't done so already, please complete exercise 21 before moving forward in this book.

Notice if you're still reading and haven't completed exercise 21. You may be encountering all kinds of personal resistance. Before Laura called Nick to address their breakdown on the beach, she needed to get through several internal barriers.

- "I don't want to share this situation with a peer because it will make me look bad."

- "I don't want to share my letter with Nick because it's a month after the argument happened, it's too weird, and he's probably busy moving across the country and starting his new job."

- "I don't want to call him and read the letter to him because I don't know what he's doing right now, and I don't want to catch him at a bad time or catch him off guard."

But she got over these barriers because she recognized that the future she wanted—for her relationship with Nick, for her own growth, and for the world—was worth it.

We have seen these techniques applied in a huge variety of contexts, from Lockheed Martin, Bose, and PricewaterhouseCoopers (PwC) to the US Navy. This is what Brent Segal, a research and development executive at Lockheed Martin, reported:

I had gotten stuck with a VP of my company as I repeatedly proposed a change of course for a major project. In the workshop, I saw that I had been arrogant and overbearing in these conversations, and I decided to try being calm, listening, and welcoming. Literally the next day, a fifteen-minute planned meeting with him stretched to forty-five and a bargain was struck.

These are the kinds of stories that inspired this book. When conversations are no longer a barrier, anything seems possible.

chapter 6 summary

- Bringing conversations back to life starts with acknowledging our baggage and bait and apologizing for how we got the conversation stuck.

- We sometimes resist apologizing because we believe that apologies give up our power. In fact, they create power by making ourselves responsible and by strengthening our relationships.

- People may not immediately change their behavior and perspective in response to our apology, but an opening is created. The apology moves the conversation from being stuck by the past to creating a future together.

- Because acknowledging a pitfall will make you feel especially vulnerable, it takes a special level of commitment and accountability with your buddy to get into action. The results will be worth it.

- *Do the work*: Role-play a conversation where you share the details of the pitfall you have been in, and apologize. Then commit to and take action—go engage with the person and bring the conversation back to life.

7

Embrace the Tension
How our differences can
make a difference

Up until now, we have been working with you to get unstuck. If you are practicing the exercises, you have brought a conversation back to life that had previously been stuck. You named and acknowledged your old way of being and bait, perhaps in an explicit and public way. You shared what is meaningful and important to you, as well as the future you want to create for your relationship and the wider world. We expect this has helped you and the other person in the conversation to break through old patterns and begin moving forward together.

You may also notice other contexts in your life and work where you have no personal history of getting stuck, pre-existing pitfalls, or baggage. You're not stuck yet, and you'd prefer it stayed that way. Yet there is still some bridge to cross, some tension between how you see the world and how (you think) "they" see the world. Perhaps you are part of a group, organization, or political party that has a polarized history with them, even if you haven't personally been involved. Perhaps they have an expectation or stereotype about how you are going to be, and you have an expectation about how they are going to be. In those contexts you want to avoid pitfalls and instead have conversations that are authentic, powerful, engaging, and creative from the start.

The goal of this chapter is to teach you how to produce creative, positive outcomes anywhere with people across various lines. The key premise is this: we might think the tensions between "us" and "them" are a barrier to creative solutions, but in fact, the possibility for innovation and flourishing emerges from embracing the tension.

Think of the polarization between different points of view as potential energy. When it is fully charged, we avoid it because we don't want to get zapped. But when we bring the charge down just enough, it can be very useful. It can fuel motion and creativity. To harness that power, we offer four steps for approaching new (or renewed) conversations in a polarized world:

1. Clarify values: Get beyond factual debates, and seek to understand the emotional truth of the conversation: what you each care most about.

2. Own the polarization: Acknowledge how you, your group, and others in your movement have contributed to a historical sense of trade-off, conflict, and polarization between those values. Confront your own inner tensions and ambivalence.

3. Expand the landscape: Declare an intention to break apparent trade-offs between values.

4. Dance in the new terrain: Brainstorm, search, connect, prototype, and create beyond the existing boundaries.

These steps are explained in the following sections.

Clarify values

When we get stuck with the bait of right, righteous, certain, and safe, our conversations tend to focus on the *facts or content* of what people are saying. For example, both of us have politically conservative relatives who will say things like "I don't believe man-made climate change is real, and I think it's an excuse for bigger government intrusion in the economy." Our knee-jerk reaction is to argue with the factual content of this statement: to tell them why they are wrong about the science and prove to them that temperatures are rising, the weather is getting crazier, and human-driven greenhouse gas emissions are causing both. We find ourselves being rationalistic, argumentative, and frustrated. We ask questions that attempt to poke holes in their argument, like "What are your sources for that?"

Often, the tone of the conversation stays combative and defensive because they hear the subtext of our question, which sounds to them like "You don't know what you are talking about." At best, if we get through this, we'll get a bunch of links and books in our in-box in support of "their side."

Let's pay attention to a different part of our relatives' statement: "Climate change is an excuse for bigger government intrusion in the economy." Lurking in this part of the statement is something beyond facts. Here they are exposing their *values*. What if we directed our attention toward that?

They have a future they want to create. They care about opportunity and liberty, a future where people live free of government domination. If scientists and environmentalists are telling them to give that up to tackle climate change, it will be a tough pill to swallow.[1] Yet we can lean into that value for ourselves. We too want a future of opportunity and freedom—*and* we want to mitigate climate change. Since we want both, that's where a creative design space emerges.

People's values are organized around spheres of care

Many models are available to help clarify underlying values. First we want to introduce our *spheres of care*. Spheres of care help articulate the scope of our aspirations for various *parts* and *wholes* of social life. Conversations "to create a better world" are always about the fate of wholes: whole school systems, whole companies, whole value chains, whole governments, whole societies, whole ecosystems, the whole planet. But those wholes are made up of parts, which are usually people, groups of people, or pieces of infrastructure and ecosystems that particular people care about. If we care about the future of a system, it is usually because we are a part of that system, or people we care about are part of that system. Figure 4 shows nested layers of parts-in-wholes, from me as an individual all the way to "all life."

Issues, advocates, and movements arise because contradictions or conflicts are perceived between the interests of the individual and the interests of the collective, the part and the whole. Here are some examples:

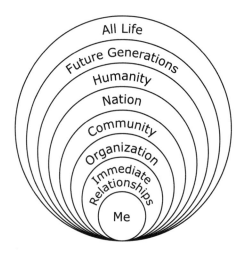

Figure 4 Spheres of care

- It may be safe and convenient for my child to skip his or her immunizations, as long as all the other children get theirs, but if we all opt out, dangerous epidemics occur and many children become sick.

- It may be faster for me to get to work in my car than by bus or bicycle, but if everyone acts like me, we get traffic jams, underinvestment in public transit and bicycle infrastructure, and longer commuting times for everyone.

- We may want each decision about school admissions and employment to be based on individual merit, but those decisions can add up to reinforce patterns of inequality in society.

In the context of conflict, consider which sphere of care is most important to you and to the person you're in conflict with. Is there a situation where caring for one whole seems to require compromising the liberty of a *part* of that whole? Once you've identified the tension, we will help you harness the creative potential.

Exercise 22
Your values, their values

Write down some of your own values.

- What really matters to you in the context of the conversation, the relationship, and your life more generally? Build on your work from the exercises in chapter 5.

- Where would you locate your values in the spheres of care? Whom do you stand for? What parts or wholes are you most passionate about protecting and nurturing? Name the specific community, place, or group.

- What qualities do you most want the broader system (organization, community, society) to embody?

- What is most sacred to you?

Now apply this analysis to the person you hope to engage.

- Write down what you think the other person most values. Articulate these values in a positive frame—what the person is *for* (rather than *against*).

What is this person's sphere of care? How and where does the person express personal values?

As you start listing the person's values in a positive way, you may be surprised to find yourself agreeing or resonating with those values.

One of our participants working on global sustainability faced resistance from his company's chief financial officer. In considering the CFO's values, he had an epiphany:

> He actually thinks about sustainability every day. What he really values and cares about is the sustainability of the company. If we aren't financially solvent into the future, we won't be able to achieve any goals, sustainability or otherwise.

What emerged out of this realization? A newfound commitment to understand the economic costs and benefits—the business case—of an environmental initiative in the company. From there, he was able to generate a new approach.

Own the polarization

Once you have identified the different values in the conversation, the next step is to acknowledge how those values can become polarized and your own role in that process. This step requires a bit more vulnerability and authenticity, but it can also be the most fun.

Consider the spheres-of-care model we presented in figure 4. Given the conflicts that occur, we often experience parts and wholes as two opposite poles, as shown in figure 5.

Figure 5 Trade-offs between parts and wholes

This view of the world suggests a kind of trade-off, balance, or choice between the needs of the individual and the needs of the collective. Within this trade-off perspective, we take sides: either I will protect my freedom to drive, eat, and enjoy my property, or I will sacrifice and be a bus-riding vegetarian and take a reduced salary to work for a nonprofit. Does this sound familiar?

When this is our mental model, the way we see the world, sometimes the best outcome we can envision is a "compromise"—a halfway point or middle ground, as shown in figure 6. We see this happen quite a bit in the commercial sphere. Have you ever used a "green cleaning" product that didn't do quite as good a job taking mildew off a shower tile? Have you ever driven an "energy efficient" car that felt anemic when you hit the accelerator pedal? We bought both of those products! (And we've left less-than-sparkling showers at home and driven around town in our hybrids while feeling self-righteous for making the compromise.)

Value 1 ⟵————————✕————————⟶ Value 2

"Compromise"

Figure 6 When we perceive a fundamental trade-off between values, the best we can imagine is compromising one for the other

Now, let's acknowledge how the solutions of the past may have forced people to choose between these values or to compromise on one of their values to enjoy another. When we can only imagine behaviors, products, and policies that require a trade-off, our conversations will get stuck debating between them. I will likely find myself telling you what you should want, justifying why you should give up on your values to come closer to mine, and I fall into the pitfall of self-righteousness. Add up whole groups and movements of people taking that approach, and you get the cultural polarization we all suffer.

Owning the polarization means first acknowledging this history, validating that there is an underlying idea of a trade-off or zero-sum game and a precedent for why that idea exists. Then it means acknowledging our ambivalence. Given the opportunity, do I want to choose between my life and all life, between product performance and impact, or between my child and all children? Rather than arguing for one over the other, I would honestly like both.

Acknowledging our ambivalence can be difficult. You may even have a strong aversion to the word "ambivalence." It comes from the Latin *ambi*, meaning "both," and *valentia*, meaning "strength." Sometimes we're so dug in to one side, while making the other side wrong, that seeing beyond polarization takes serious internal reflection. But when we can see both values as valid, even desirable, and acknowledge our role in the polarization, something different becomes possible.

The spheres-of-care model is meant to help you articulate and broaden your perspective. It is not a comprehensive model. However, it illustrates the tensions you'll be navigating if you're out to create a better world. You can see that your own life flourishing is part of all life flourishing, and yet they are also seemingly at odds with each other. Similarly, my success is bound up in and at odds with the success of my organization. Once we can see these relationships, it's easier to recognize that the solutions we really want will break classical trade-offs and contribute to both values or objectives.

Values differ across political lines

In *politically* charged conversations, it can be helpful to enrich the spheres-of-care model by thinking about the "moral foundations" that underlie our parties and ideologies. Social psychologist Jonathan Haidt suggests that humans are wired to care about six moral values: care, liberty, fairness, loyalty, authority, and sanctity.[2] While there are systematic differences in how liberals, libertarians, and conservatives prioritize and understand these values, each value is innate within each of us. Thus, when exploring what's important, you might ask: What do they find sacred? And what do we find sacred? Whose liberty do they want to protect? And whose liberty do we want to protect? Whom do we each want to care for or treat fairly? To whom do we want to express loyalty, and what authority structures do we each consider to be important?

On the streets of Cleveland during the 2016 Republican National Convention, just before Donald Trump was about to be nominated as the Republican candidate for president, Owen Shroyer saw Van Jones walk past a bar where he was sitting. Shroyer was from Infowars, a news organization that stood for libertarian and constitutionalist ideas, representing the far political right. Jones founded several social and environmental justice organizations and served as President Obama's special advisor for green jobs. He also was cast as the liberal pundit on CNN's show *Crossfire*. The encounter happened amid nationwide clashes between police and protestors over the question of racial bias in the criminal justice system.

Shroyer and his cameraman jumped up from their drinks and ran down the sidewalk after Jones, asking him on camera to do an interview. Jones responded to specific questions about race and racism while dodging heckling from passing Trump supporters. Along the way he expressed several great examples of ambivalence and his relationship with Shroyer transformed.[3]

So, this is beautiful. I didn't run from you. I didn't not talk to you. Because this is what we're supposed to do. I didn't go get a gun, you didn't go get a gun. I didn't call you a name, you didn't call me a name. We can argue back and forth. . . . The only way this thing works is if you cry just as much when that black man dies in that police car and I cry just as much when that horrible bigoted sniper shot down those police. If you're crying over those funerals and I'm crying over those funerals and we're both crying together, we can find a way to get our cops to be better and to get our kids to be better. . . .

No one leader . . . has all the answers. Neither political party has all of the answers. When the country works right, the Republicans bring something to the table. They say, "How much does this cost and who's going to pay for it?" That's a good thing for Republicans to ask. Republicans ask, "Should the government be doing this any dadgum way?" That's a good thing for the Republicans to ask. The Democrats say . . . ," "Can you have a country that works only by doing what corporations can make money off of? What about other stuff?" That's good for us to bring. We ask the question, "What about those subgroups that might get run over by the big majorities?" Those are good questions. . . . When we come together the right way, Republicans talk about liberty, individual freedom, limited government. Democrats talk about justice, what about those little guys getting run over? Liberty and justice for all. That's America. That's how it's supposed to be. . . . What's happening now is, if you're for liberty, I call you a racist. If I'm for justice, you call me a socialist. . . . That's gotta stop.

At the end of the interview, Shroyer turned to the camera and said, "I've got to be honest. I've been one of the biggest haters of Van Jones, probably on the Internet, and I'm gonna go ahead and walk back some of my hate for Van Jones." He then suggested Jones could come to Infowars to share his ideas with an audience outside his liberal circles.

We use the Van Jones story to illustrate that we are not asking you to simply reframe or cloak your values in language that you think the other person cares about. We are asking you to internalize someone else's values (as you are asking the other person to do). Initially, we suggest you use these tools to explore what matters to you. By acknowledging your own ambivalence, you'll be better equipped to navigate conversations with people you traditionally don't agree with. And by training this muscle, you can learn to do it in real time in conversations that could otherwise be adversarial. We will show you how to use a diversity of values, especially values seemingly in conflict, as a source of flourishing and innovation.

Exercise 23
Your values, their values (continued)

Consider your own values and those of the person or group you hope to engage. Use the spheres-of-care and moral foundations models if useful. Make two lists: *my values* and *their values*.

Now, consider when or how what they value has been important in your own life. Consider where you may have stood for what they value, perhaps in another context. Where do you have common ground? What values, if any, seem irreconcilable?

Make some notes in response to these questions about how your values relate to theirs.

Consider having a dialogue with the person or group members about your values and theirs:

- Ask them whether you have accurately understood their values and how they would describe them.

- Share situations where their values resonate with you.

- Ask them which of your values resonate with them as well.

- Explore what might seem fundamentally at odds.

Expand the landscape

Once we start to acknowledge both our values and the other person's values as valid, as well as the history of trade-off and polarization, it becomes time to change the basic assumption in the conversation. Rather than seeing the world in one polarized dimension, we can create a two-dimensional conversation.

Sean Kenney and Rob Wilson at MFS Investment Management faced a conundrum. They had been working to help both MFS's investment team and MFS's clients more thoroughly integrate the analysis of environmental, social, and governance (ESG) criteria into their investment decision-making processes. Their goal was to find companies that would outperform in the market (performance) and better manage their social and environmental risks and opportunities (impact). When they went to engage their clients—pension funds, endowments, and other institutional investors—they found themselves repeatedly hearing opposition: "We don't do socially responsible investment. We have a fiduciary responsibility to maximize the returns of our portfolio." In essence, people weren't buying the "win-win" argument. They believed there must be a strong trade-off between the economic performance and social impact of the investment strategy, as illustrated in figure 7.

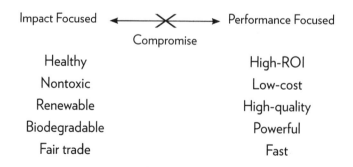

Figure 7 A one-dimensional conversation in the corporate and investing world

This mental model of a trade-off is very common and is a pervasive background conversation that halts sustainability efforts.

> Sean and Rob recognized that arguing "There is no trade-off" to people who believed "There is always a trade-off" wasn't getting them anywhere.
>
> Instead, as they engaged their clients, Sean and Rob showed a slide depicting a graph of return on investment (ROI) versus social value as not just one dimension but two dimensions: a rational, long-term-oriented investor should care about both social impact and performance. They drew a downward-sloping trade-off line (the more social value, the less return) similar to the one shown in figure 8. They said, "This is a very common way of seeing the investment landscape. And in fact it's true. There are investments that would get a lower return with more social impact, and vice versa." They even gave examples to validate this point of view. These included the immediate negative impact that higher wages could have on near-term financial results, and a high short-term return from investments in toxic industries if externalities are not properly managed by society.[4]
>
> "And," they said, "it's also true that we could imagine shifting this line outward—finding clever investment strategies that could break the trade-offs. We could do that by paying attention to information that other investors aren't paying attention to." At this point, they showed examples of how well-designed environmental and socially informed strategies can outperform the financial benchmarks.

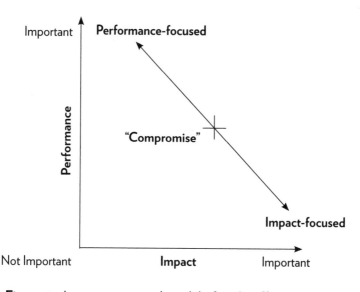

Figure 8 A common mental model of trade-offs
between performance and impact

We depict this shift in figure 9 as a push into new territory beyond the frontier of perceived trade-offs. Doing
this requires innovation but it moves in the direction of
flourishing—achieving benefits for individuals, companies, and society.

The results were significant: the MFS team's clients
responded positively to this conversation and began
seriously considering their ESG approach. The conversation created an opening where one had not existed
before.

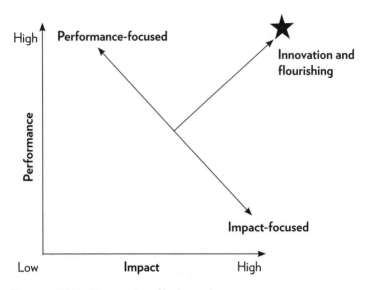

Figure 9 Breaking trade-offs through innovation

We can look at this pathway as a rhetorical strategy:

- Describe the implicit "trade-off" or "either-or" mental model.

- Validate it with examples to show that you understand its basis.

- Invite the other person to consider a space of possibilities beyond the trade-off.

- Together, consider options in that space and how well they meet "both-and" goals.

Of course, trade-off-breaking "both-and" solutions won't always be apparent. But you can navigate your way into the conversational space where those solutions could possibly be uncovered. This is the creative frontier that is possible only by being in dialogue with people who will challenge you to expand your value set.

Exercise 24
Go beyond a one-dimensional conversation

Where do you experience the most tension around the idea of making the world a better place?

First draw the tension as a single line, a trade-off between two things you value or one thing that you value and something that "other people" value, as shown in figure 10. The poles could be abstract ideals like individual rights versus the collective good, liberty versus justice, or economic growth versus environmental protection. They could be social groups like urban people of color versus rural whites. They could be different spheres of care like my department versus the whole organization.

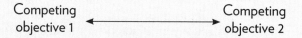

Competing
objective 1

Competing
objective 2

Figure 10 Competing objectives

Do you find yourself oscillating from one side to the other? Have you made one side "right" and the other "wrong"? Have you made the people who embody one side or the other "right" or "wrong" as a result?

Now redraw the picture as a two-dimensional space, with one value on the horizontal axis and one on the vertical axis, as shown in figure 11.

Continued on next page

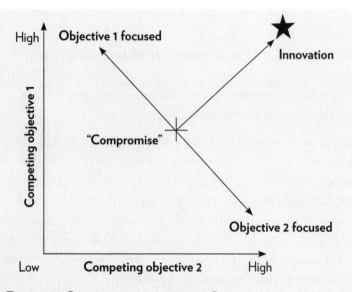

Figure 11 Compromise or innovation?

What "solutions" have actually been compromises, asking people to give up on one objective to achieve another? These might be habits, products, strategies, or policies.

Allow yourself to imagine pushing out the frontier, exploring the space of innovation marked by the star in figure 11. Can you let yourself believe that something out there might be possible? If you imagine that breaking the trade-off might be possible, does that make it easier to acknowledge the importance of both values?

If your drawing represents a tension between your objectives and those of another person, how might you take that other person on this same journey of acknowledging the polarization, acknowledging compromises, and expanding the landscape?

Dance in the new terrain

You may notice that this approach looks like an iterative process of innovation—considering a space of possibility, generating options, and evaluating them. In fact, that is the fundamental opportunity here. We can shift the focus from the past and present, where people believe trade-offs are required, to a focus on a future we can create together. We can use multiple competing values as drivers of creativity and innovation.

- -

Exercise 25
Brainstorm ideas that break trade-offs between values and objectives

Where do you or others in your organization or movement experience trade-offs between multiple values or objectives? In this domain, when have you heard people cynically argue that "both-and" opportunities are impossible or naively argue that they are everywhere?

First, make a list of examples in your context that validate the trade-off: solutions that were high on one value but low on the other.

Now, share your examples with someone who has argued on one side or the other, and acknowledge that the trade-off exists. If you have been right, righteous, certain, or safe in your own views, acknowledge this too!

Finally, acknowledge that a possible space of "both-and" could be carefully considered and evaluated. What search or brainstorming process would help uncover new ideas in that space?

Explore together how you could evaluate those ideas against multiple competing values. Use the frameworks in the "Clarify values" section above as a guide.

When families, organizations, communities, and governments are stuck in gridlock, it is often because the existing solutions are too strong a compromise for all involved. Breaking through requires new ideas. If we can come together across the lines, clarify what matters most, and embrace the tension between values, we might generate optimal outcomes we never before envisioned. The fuel for that journey, amazingly enough, may be the same polarization that seems to keep us stuck.

chapter 7 summary

- You can turn polarization into energy for innovation and action. Doing so requires embracing the tension between values.

- Embracing the tension involves four steps. These steps can help you move forward from a stuck conversation—after you have done the hard work of acknowledging your own pitfalls. They can also help you approach new conversations in a polarized context.

- The first step is to move beyond factual debates and *clarify values*, as well as associated hopes and fears. Consider spheres of care and moral foundations in understanding other perspectives.

- The second step is to *own the polarization*. Acknowledge your own ambivalence—the concern you have for the other person's values. And acknowledge when you have contributed to polarization in the past.

- The third step is to *expand the landscape*. Declare an intention to move beyond compromises that satisfy neither party's goals and to find solutions that break apparent trade-offs between values.

- The last step is to *dance in the new terrain*. Brainstorm, search, connect, prototype, and create beyond the familiar ideas.

- *Do the work*: Use the exercises in this chapter to engage someone whose values or strategies appear to be in tension with your own. This could be in a conversation that is newly unstuck as a result of your work in chapters 3 through 6, or it could be with a new person or group you want to engage.

8

Widen the Circle
Building inclusive
movements

Remember the story about migrant labor activist Cesar Chavez back in chapter 1? He built his movement by talking to one person, then another person, and then another person. Inspired by that idea, this book has focused on interpersonal conversations, helping you engage people one by one, beyond "preaching to the choir" of people who agree with you.

Fundamentally, there is no shortcut. You can't change collective conversations without changing individual conversations. As we'll see, however, your individual conversations will train and prepare you for changing a larger conversation. Using the tools of this book, you can widen the circle of inquiry and impact.

Gabriel shared his recycling story as a personal example at a green business conference in 2015. A director at a major automotive company said, "We've re-created your recycling conversation with tens of thousands of people." Gabriel asked what that looked like, and the director said, "Well, for instance, we know that when we send out a communication about oily-rag contamination in the cardboard recycling, contamination goes up. We have data on that. But we still send out those communications. Our e-mails have likely discouraged thousands of people from doing something they perhaps previously enjoyed contributing toward. I've already scheduled a meeting for our team. We're going to change that immediately."

Remember the story about Laura and her friend Nick in chapter 6—how she learned to have a courageous and vulnerable conversation about climate change? Here is the next chapter of that story:

> During a summer internship with the Indiana state gov-
> ernment in 2015, I had the opportunity to meet Vice
> President Mike Pence, who was the Republican gov-
> ernor of Indiana at the time. He hosted a reception in
> his office for about thirty interns from the Governor's
> Public Service Summer Internship program, including
> me. For years, then governor Pence had been a very
> vocal opponent of the EPA's Clean Power Plan, and he
> wasn't known for supporting the environment. In the
> past, I would have avoided engaging with him. I proba-
> bly would have skipped the reception, having thoughts
> like "It's not worth my time" or "I couldn't possibly have
> an impact." That way of being would have been self-
> fulfilling, whether I decided to engage or not.
>
> Based on my experience with Nick, I showed up em-
> bodying compassion and understanding. I asked Pence
> a question about the future of Indiana's environmental
> leadership and, to my surprise, he asked for my opinion. I
> told him I was working toward graduate degrees in pub-
> lic policy and environmental science because I was com-
> mitted to protecting human and environmental health.

I shared about an Indiana program I was proud of that provides small businesses with free technical support in navigating complex environmental regulations, ensuring economic success and environmental health.

To the wild surprise of my colleagues and me, he was inspired to give an impromptu speech to our entire class of interns on the beauty of Indiana's natural resources and the importance of environmental stewardship at the highest levels of state government. It was the most pro-environment speech I've heard from Pence, delivered to a group of people who will likely be making important policy decisions in years to come.

A year later, then governor Pence was traveling the country, campaigning for vice president alongside Donald Trump. After a mention of climate change in the first presidential debate, Trump's campaign manager issued a statement saying Trump "does not believe global warming is a man-made phenomenon." During a CNN interview later that week, Pence was asked by Chris Cuomo about the Trump campaign's position on global warming, and he responded: "There's no question that the activities that take place in this country and in countries around the world have some impact on the environment and some impact on climate."[1]

I was shocked by this declaration, which directly contradicted a core policy position of Trump and the GOP leadership. I can't know whether our conversation at the intern reception produced any direct policy outcomes or how much it influenced Pence's personal beliefs. What I can say is that I am so profoundly grateful that I decided to show up that day and have a difficult conversation.

Start where you are. As you take on conversations with those who are closest to you, you'll learn how to unlock the conversations the world needs unlocked. You'll build confidence and discover new pathways forward you can share with others. Maybe you'll create a whole language for your cause, like John at HPE with trainings and materials, or perhaps you'll inspire an entire industry to transform, like Melissa and Joyce at Interface. Know that there is someone whom only you could possibly reach, perhaps someone who will be voting in the next election or moving into a position of influence. You need not get too hung up on where to start practicing. First you talk to one person, then another person.

Shared inquiry is required to change the collective conversation

At some point, however, you may want to pull back and see what this could look like on a collective scale.

What happens when groups of people or whole movements fall into pitfalls? What would be possible if people in our movements systematically let go of the bait, brought conversations back to life, and embraced tensions in a creative way? What new conversations would emerge and define our movements? What would be people's experience of us? What outcomes would become possible?

Our goal in this book is to create pathways together to break through gridlock and polarization. Just as our pitfalls and tensions can be inherited and transcend us, so can our pathways forward. A *pathway* takes us from a specific set of individual conversations to collective conversations that become possible through their accumulation and to powerful collective outcomes. To get there, we'll apply the tools of this book to a wider context: identifying core tensions and pitfalls, working to embrace and transform them, and taking constructive action to create a new discourse.

Throughout this chapter, we will build on our own experience in the sustainability movement and our reflections on the tensions and pitfalls we are familiar with. Our intention, however, is for our example to be relevant to other movements and conversations. We have seen parallels with people fighting for social justice (e.g., education and criminal justice reform) and for public health and safety (e.g., healthcare reform and campaigns dealing with smoking, obesity, and gun violence). The processes in this chapter are relevant to leaders in any movement that is driven by a vision for a better world and that cannot succeed without getting beyond polarization and gridlock.

Each social movement has core tensions and pitfalls

What does it mean to take the pitfalls-and-tensions perspective from individual conversations to a whole movement?

Let's consider what happens when we assemble a whole crowd of people and organizations that have taken a stand for sustainability. Here is our experience. We are wrestling with a core set of tensions:

- We care for ourselves and the poor in the current moment who seem best served by inclusive economic growth. But we also care for our children and grandchildren (and those of the poor) whose well-being may be undermined by growth that destroys the environment.

- We care for oppressed people and species that we want to protect with standards, rules, and regulations. But we also want the freedom to make our own choices as consumers and businesspeople.

- We want to reduce our consumption and selectively buy products, services, and investments that mitigate social and environmental harm. But we also want the same performance (comfort, power, speed, etc.) that anyone in our society has come to expect.

- We want to be optimistic about the potential of human ingenuity and goodness to create a positive future. But we also look at the current state and direction of inequality and environmental degradation and feel disillusioned about that future.

In talking with colleagues immersed in other groups, movements, and collective conversations, we have heard different tensions. In healthcare reform, we often hear thoughtful practitioners say that on the one hand they want to provide the best healthcare to the patient in front of them. On the other hand, they want to spend time, money, and other resources in a way that ensures the best health outcomes for our society (even if that means holding back with an individual patient). This tension gets mapped across organizational groups and leads to friction and strife, for example, between frontline providers and financial administrators.

In social justice movements, advocates strive for *representativeness*. An organization pursuing criminal justice reform should have formerly incarcerated individuals and people of color at the helm, ensuring they have voices and are contributing directly to their own empowerment. At the same time, there is no guarantee that these directly impacted people will have an effective strategy for change. Furthermore, white Ivy League lawyers and consultants often have an easier time raising money and building partnerships with other elites. As a result, organizations that maximize representativeness may be perceived as not having the capacity for systemic change. Swinging the other direction, an organization maximizing *effectiveness* might believe it has to give up representativeness and hire people from privileged backgrounds. In so doing, however, it faces serious critiques from the grass roots about its legitimacy: "Those people don't speak for us."

Frictions arise among people with complementary or common goals and can diminish everyone's energy and cohesive impact. At the center is a tension between representativeness and effectiveness, between the health of the individual and the health of the whole, or between being visionary and being realistic. Yet we need to build organizations and coalitions that are *both* representative *and* effective at making change. We need strategies that draw from the unique capabilities of marginalized *and* privileged groups. We contribute toward the health of the whole by caring for the individuals. And we need visionary approaches that are well grounded in current realities.

These are core tensions at the heart of our movements. When expressed in a healthy way, these tensions drive our learning and innovation. They give our pursuits meaning and purpose. They inspire engagement and pathways forward. Too often we instead let these tensions turn into polarization within ourselves, between organizations, and on the wider political stage. The tensions become sources of resignation and cynicism, frustration and burnout. They create divisiveness outside the choir and infighting within. They become the source of our pitfalls.

Realist-visionary tensions are present in all social movements

First, we'll expand on a tension between realist and visionary perspectives that we have seen in all social movements we have encountered. Consider for a moment exercise 24 in chapter 7 on creating two-dimensional conversations. In a one-dimensional conversation, you're either a realist or a visionary. From the perspective of a realist, what we need is incremental change. The realist has heard people talk about vision, and yet, looking back, sees that all change is incremental. From the perspective of the visionary, what we need is transformative change. Incremental change is inadequate for the problems at hand, and we can't possibly get where we want to go without first being able to imagine it. The realist sees the visionary as delusional, and the visionary sees the realist as disillusioned. You could say delusion and disillusion are two pitfalls that emerge from the tension between being realistic and being visionary.

In practice, when the realist hears a visionary conversation, he's tempted to interject, to represent the "voice of reality." When the visionary hears realism, she thinks "a bigger perspective" is needed. What ensues is a one-dimensional debate or oscillation, each person reaffirming to the other that his or her perspective is even more needed. Polarization ensues.

The truth is, we are all visionaries, and we are all realists. You may find yourself arguing for one unrepresented perspective in one group and the other in another. You may grow to be known as the realist in one community and the visionary in another yet fail to create the impact you want in either conversation.

A pathway emerges when we step from a one-dimensional visionary-versus-realist space into a two-dimensional conversation. When both perspectives are present, we have healthy creative tension.[2] We create a possibility space that is both grounded in current reality and has access to the power of vision.

As an example, consider this additional excerpt from the Van Jones Infowars interview that transformed Jones's relationship with Owen Shroyer, which we shared in chapter 7.

> If we're going to be one country, and . . . we've got no choice, we've got every color, every category, every gender, every sexuality, every faith, every kind of human being ever born living in the United States. We are a miracle in the history of humanity. There's no country that's ever even tried to do what we do every day in this country. You've got countries that have got two ethnic groups and they can't get along with two. . . .

But now among Americans, we have to be honest. America has always been two things and not one thing. We start out with that great founding reality that was disappointing even to the founders. You go to the Jefferson memorial, Thomas Jefferson in marble and stone says, "I tremble for my country when I reflect that God is just" . . . he's talking about slavery. . . . That is a founding reality. . . . But the good thing is that there is also the founding dream. That same Thomas Jefferson said, "We hold these truths to be self-evident, that all are created equal."

Now that's America. The ugly founding reality . . . and that beautiful dream. And what makes us Americans is that we have a process of debate, of amendment, to close that gap, every generation, a little bit more, between that founding reality and that founding dream. That's what makes us Americans. . . . So if you make the mistake of [denying] that founding dream and just look at the ugliness of that founding reality, you're wrong. We're more than just that founding reality. But if, on the other hand, you won't look at that founding reality and you won't look at the pain of people whose immediate family members suffered in that founding reality, and you tell us that we're wrong, you also don't get the joke, you also don't understand America.

If you have stuck with us so far, you are already holding this visionary-realist tension. The letter-writing exercise we shared with you in chapter 6 is an interpersonal exercise that guided you through communicating both the current reality and your vision more powerfully than you had before. The current reality is your relationship to the bait (chapter 4), and the vision is what you really want (chapter 5). Sharing either of those, alone, would fall short of inviting the conversation into a space of healthy creative tension.

In this chapter we'll invite you to build on this skill to create multidimensional spaces of healthy creative tension for your movement. The first step is to identify your movement's core tensions.

Exercise 26
Core tensions in your movement

Gather a small group of people in your organization or movement (this could be you and your buddy), and consider the following questions:

- What are the central tensions in your movement? What are the tensions or contradictory desires you often hear expressed within your movement?

- What are the tensions or values that separate the people in your movement from those outside it?

Write each tension you identify, putting each value in positive terms, that is, what people are standing for (rather than what they're against).

It may take some time to articulate what those outside your movement are standing for. It's common for us to settle for "they're against what we want" rather than doing the work to understand what they are for. If you get stuck, ask someone who disagrees with you for the answer.

If you are in the sustainability movement, consider our reflections. What might you add? Edit our words to fit your experience.

Movements can have collective bait and pitfalls

How do we let go of the bait and embrace the tension at a movement level? In chapters 3 through 7, transforming a conversation and bringing it back to life was something that you could do as an individual. You personally have the power of reflecting on your conversation and courageously re-engaging. Releasing a collective pitfall is partly a matter of doing exactly that and changing a series of individual conversations. But you can also look at the collective conversation and *discourse* as a whole. In releasing the collective bait and climbing out of a collective pitfall, it can be helpful to take a close look at the words people use such as "sustainability," "social justice," and "public health," which become tags of identity and loyalty as well as intellectual ideas. We want to suggest that the building blocks of bait and pitfalls exist inside these very ideas and in the broader idea of a "better world."

Consider that any vision or movement for a "better world," is not one thing. What we are playing with is a vision for a whole system. Systems are made up of collections of elements—teams and organizations of people, communities of people and infrastructure, value chains, nations, ecological systems, and the planet as a whole. Very often those assemblies of elements are complex: large numbers of elements interact in a large variety of ways. "Sustainability" describes something about how the whole system works. We can't understand the sustainability of the system by looking at the behavior or health of only a part of the system. Similarly, "social justice" and "public health" are whole-system visions.

Notice that if I care about the future of a system, it is usually because I am a part of that system, or people I care about are part of that system. In the context of climate change, Jason and Gabriel both live in coastal cities. We have family living in precarious places like the coast of Florida and near Bangladesh. You may have an uncle who farms in California's Central Valley and worries about drought or a friend in the coal industry who worries about climate regulations. All of us, when we try to act on whole systems, are acting as parts of the whole.

Now consider the temptation to be right, righteous, certain, and safe in this context—the common forms of bait we identified in chapter 4.

Letting go of "right"

When I am a part of a system, how much of the system do I really get to see? How well do I really understand the thoughts going through someone's mind when she is addicted to an intravenous drug and deciding whether to reuse a needle and risk the spread of disease? How well do I understand the experience of a young black man trying to survive in a city that fears him *and* the experience of a police officer's spouse who hopes he will come home safe each day? Do I really know the motivations and perspectives of Florida homeowners when they build, buy, and insure their homes on an increasingly vulnerable coastline? As a part of a system, I have only a limited perspective on the whole.

Sometimes my view of the situation will align with others' views, and sometimes it won't. If I am holding on to the need to *be right*, I am in fact almost certainly wrong because I can't understand the situation in its full complexity. And because I'm sure that I'm right, I won't engage others whose perspectives could expand and contribute toward my own.

At the same time, what if we were to give up being right? We would have to act according to our values without knowing we were taking the "right" action. We would have to express ourselves without knowing our words are the "right" words. What would we do? What would we say? Would we act at all? This uncertainty may feel like an uncomfortable place, but allowing it is a key step on the pathway. It drives us from advocacy to inquiry: to ask questions, to listen, and to understand new perspectives.

Most of the time, however, we just act as though we're right, and the world keeps turning. You can see how being right (and making others wrong) is sticky bait when we're striving to create a better world.

Letting go of "righteous"

In each of the examples above, you or I have a particular stake in the system. I care about my ability to eat fish, you care about your uncle in California, we care about our grandkids' ability to enjoy a comfortable life. As a part of a system, I care about my part as well as the whole.

Sometimes my self-interests (particularly the long-term ones) are aligned with the health of the whole system, aka "a better world." My kids will get to eat fish too if the fishery is sustainable. But sometimes my individual interests and others' interests, or the collective interests, are in conflict. I want to eat fish now or take long hot showers, or whatever your guilty pleasure, even though I know it might undermine the system as a whole, particularly if we all do it. In this context of inner ambivalence and conflict, and interpersonal conflict, how do we cope? The more righteous I feel, the less I need to reflect on my own multiple motives or to consider whether my pursuit of my goals might be imposing on others' pursuit of theirs.

What would it look like for your group or movement to give up being righteous? How would we keep ourselves motivated? Again, we invite you to sit in that place of uncertainty and inquiry. Try to understand what positive values motivate people on "the other side."

Letting go of "certain"

Consider our quest to feel certain inside movements to make change in complex systems and societies. The future of a complex system is inherently uncertain. How many times have our predictions failed to come true? How many times have we averted an environmental catastrophe? Or are we merely postponing it and making it larger? The future is all the more uncertain in a complex system, where we have limited information about the present and where small changes can have large ripple effects. Are we inventing new means to farm salmon for the masses, or are we creating a "Trojan horse" species that could destroy entire fisheries? To say with full confidence that my lifestyle or my company's product is "sustainable," meaning that it is aligned with the sustainability of the whole, is to assume you know the future.

Nonetheless, we want a lot of people to adopt a lot of solutions if we are going to change the course of the whole system. That makes appearing certain about the problems and the benefits of our suggested solutions seem all the more important. In some cases, this approach is successful: when people are fearful and uncertain about the future, we want to provide a clear comforting answer. What does it feel like to admit uncertainty? What new sources of information might we seek?

Letting go of "safe"

Amid all the uncertain scenarios for the future of the system, many that we can conjure up are quite unpleasant. We try to prevent the oppression of minorities, the destabilization of societies, the bankruptcy of governments, the depletion of natural resources, the disruption of the climate, and so on.

But taking action to change the future is also incredibly risky. On a large scale, our solutions may have unintended consequences that we will not foresee. For example, corn-based ethanol, once touted as a solution to energy security concerns, had an upward effect on food prices that helped destabilize the Middle East in the 2000s, undermining security. Every course of action has risks in a complex system.

Getting to feel safe is almost always an illusion. At a personal level, the risks of action are also acute: we might find ourselves rejected. Individual "change agents" bear risk as well, and this is another example of a tension between the welfare of the parts and the welfare of the whole. The assassination of Martin Luther King Jr. is a dramatic example of risk, yet we all face risks as advocates who step out onto a more public stage. And if we don't take action, we run the very personal risk of feeling regret.

What would it look like to let go of the bait of feeling safe? What new risks might you take?

Exercise 27
Locate the collective bait

Reflect back on the core tensions of your movement (exercise 26). What are the sacred terms, such as "justice," "liberty," or "sustainability"? These are the words that you are *certain* stand for what is *right* and *righteous*. As long as someone agrees with you about the meaning and value of those ideas, you feel *safe* engaging with that person.

Now carefully consider the limitations of this idea and community. We suggest you do this as an individual and in partnership with others in your movement.

- Reconsider "right": What do your particular personal perspectives reveal about the complex system you hope to change, and what do they hide? What other perspectives on that system have you avoided listening to or seeing as potentially right from another person's vantage point? If you engaged with that person, how might it change your own sense of being right?

- Reconsider "righteous": What individual and group interests would benefit if your movement were to succeed? Who would decline or lose power, influence, and resources? Does your approach have any foreseeable negative side effects or consequences? How would confronting those undermine your claims to righteousness?

Continued on next page

- Reconsider "certain": How good are your data and analysis about cause-effect relationships in the system you hope to change? Which of your claims are founded in evidence, and which are assumptions? How many times have you run experiments using your solution, or how precisely have you modeled the impact of your strategy and activities into the future? How effective have you been at modeling and predicting outcomes in the past? How does confronting these questions affect your sense of certainty?

- Reconsider "safe": If you find your group is staying psychologically and socially safe by engaging only with allies, do you risk undermining your effectiveness? If so, what dangers in the world are you allowing to continue? What risks are you taking through inaction as well as action? If you confront those, how would that change your notion of what it means to be safe?

Find the possibility at the heart of our movements

What if we, as a community, let go of the bait? What if we see the contradictions and inauthenticity involved in acting right, righteous, certain, and safe and take a step back?

The truth is, we don't know what progress is. We don't know what it looks like. We don't have a clear shared vision for a future together, let alone a defined trajectory of how to get there, and we may never have that clarity. Progress—as a vessel that contains the future we want—means anything to everyone and therefore nothing to anyone.

What if we understand "sustainability," "social justice," or "public health" to be an empty vessel?

When we stand in this uncomfortable place, one choice is to rebrand the movement to more clearly define what we are for. For example, we could rebrand sustainability as being for regenerative systems, resilience, or flourishing. Or we could rebrand criminal justice reform as public safety and strong communities. Perhaps we could bring all of these movements together into one for health or wholeness. There are, in fact, elegant and well-argued manifestos for each of these moves.[3]

Any of these new terms, however, are vessels that will fill with their own meaning, their own collective hang-ups, their own shadows. This is because regeneration, resilience, flourishing, and wholeness are all emergent properties of whole complex systems, yet we still get to act as only parts of the whole. The bait of right, righteous, certain, and safe still lurks in any effort to mobilize behind an idea for a better world.

So, just for a moment, let's explore the choice to hold on to the empty vessel instead.

What if we see that emptiness in a different way? Rather than being a thing, what if we relate to our movements as a possibility? Consider social justice, public health, and sustainability—consider your movement— as a possibility.

Possibility lives in the present and future simultaneously. It is forever just out of your reach, and yet it is something that you create and re-create as you bring the future into the present moment. Being right, righteous, certain, or safe about a possibility is much harder. Your movement, as a possibility, is an inquiry. It's a set of questions, not answers. It's a conversation you can invite others into.

When we relate to our movement as an inquiry, rather than a fixed thing others must understand, we can use a whole host of conversations to invite others in. Rather than having to share a fixed vision, we are free to invite others into a conversation for envisioning alongside us. Rather than being embarrassed about chasing our bait, we have an opportunity to explore our humanity alongside each other together.

Exercise 28
Envision the future together

Practice crafting conversations about possibilities by inviting someone important to you into a conversation where you envision a better world. Choose someone with whom you have an existing relationship but who doesn't usually see eye to eye with you. This could be an informal get-together—for example, a shared meal or a scheduled office meeting.

What challenges does the person see that we need to overcome?

If we were to overcome those challenges, what would the world look like that the person would be excited to pass on to our grandchildren?

If the person asks, share the future you're inspired to create.

Be aware that you're crafting a creative tension, and people can have a variety of responses inside that space. They may be playfully delusional or realistic and disillusioned. Notice any tendency you have to fix or correct the person's response, and let go of it.

Practice steering the conversation toward a healthy creative tension by articulating and reflecting back both the future the person wants and the challenges that must be overcome: "Your dream is . . ." "And you fear the most insurmountable challenge is . . ."

If you've shared your own desired future, practice exploring a both-and possibility space. How would the person's vision complement yours? How might the person's goals be necessary to the future you want? How might those objectives sometimes conflict?

Notice your own ways of being inside this conversation.

In chapter 5 we shared a guided meditation and the results from our workshops when people sat through it and then shared their way of being inside the future they want to create. Those results are depicted again in figure 12.

Figure 12 Ways of being expressed inside a positive future[4]

Look at this word cloud again. What occurs when we take the bold step to let go of the bait and dwell in this space? For us, the experience recalls a thirteenth-century poem by Rumi:

*Out beyond ideas of wrongdoing and rightdoing,
there is a field. I'll meet you there.*

*When the soul lies down in that grass,
the world is too full to talk about.
Ideas, language, even the phrase "each other"
doesn't make any sense.*[5]

Standing in this place, from the ways of being in figure 3, how would you articulate the core possibility of your movement?

John Ehrenfeld, in a moment of inquiry like this, made a statement that became the basis of his writing and has inspired our work: "Sustainability is the possibility that humans and other life will flourish on Earth forever." "Flourishing" is a useful description of what the world would look like if everything works out—when we successfully unite with others and mobilize to handle the "unsustainabilities." Like us, Ehrenfeld has articulated ways that the sustainability movement has not been authentic in creating that kind of future.[5] And this creative tension between who we want to be for the world and who we have been gives us a powerful conversational starting point with people outside the movement. We can empathize with people who think we've been a bunch of holier-than-thou jerks because, well, we have been. And we can share powerfully with them what matters most to us.

Take a moment to articulate your vision or the possibility of your movement. Notice what pitfalls have emerged or where you've been inauthentic in pursuit of that possibility. How do people experience you in the world? Is that way of being consistent with the future you want? What bait holds you in past patterns? What do you gain when conversations lose? What way of being would be consistent with the future you want to create? What do you really want? Who are you willing to share that with?

While we're not suggesting you publish it, draft a letter that could inspire the transformation you want to create within your movement. This may require going through some of the earlier exercises in the book with other people in your organization and movement.

Exercise 29
Transform the central conversation of your movement

With others in your group, organization, or movement, work to fill in the blanks in the following:

As we have engaged in conversations about _____ (context for engagement and activism), we want to acknowledge that our ways of being have included _____ (old ways of being).

While we have been saying we want _____ (goals for a better future), really we were also going for _____ (baits).

We recognize some unfortunate consequences of this approach, which include _____ (consequences of being stuck).

We are sorry to have taken this approach. We want to create a new way to engage.

Continued on next page

Going forward in this conversation and relationship, you can count on us to be _____ (new ways of being), which is consistent with the future we really want, which is _____ (the possibility of the movement). And we want you to call us on it if you catch us slipping back into old habits.

Here is a story of a moment like this in the social justice movement.

In 1988, Molly Baldwin started Roca, an organization dedicated to the highest risk young people in Massachusetts, many of whom were in and out of jail. At first she saw law enforcement members as adversaries, both for the kids and for her work. Taking a stand for the youth meant taking a stand against the system that held them down. Soon, however, she started to see the limits of her approach. Youth were spending time in her programs but continuing to get in trouble. Police saw her nascent community center and after-school program as a haven for gang members and did not trust her efforts.

Molly tried holding peacekeeping circles that brought youth and police together to share their hopes and fears in a safe space. At first there was nothing safe about it. "Forty people came—young people, police and probation officers, community members, and friends," recalls Molly. "Halfway through the opening session, everything blew up. People were screaming, the kids were swearing, everyone was saying, 'See! This is never going to work!' Watching the session break down was wrenching, but eventually I understood how committed I was to divisiveness and not unity, how far I was from being a peacemaker. I understood on a visceral level the problems with 'us and them' thinking, and how I perpetuated that, personally and for the organization. Continuing to insist, 'I'm right, you're wrong! The issue is you, not us, because we hold the moral high ground!' was a big source of what was limiting our ability to truly help people and situations."[7]

Molly and her team approached the chief of police and shared these reflections, acknowledging their role in the conflict. Starting with that moment, the relationship shifted to a different footing. Subsequent peacekeeping circles gradually became more and more able to create real dialogue. "We have come a long way in terms of our work with the police in all the cities we are privileged to serve. Authentic and meaningful conversations with cops at all ranks are not 'nice to have'—they are an inseparable part of helping high-risk young people change their lives. It takes time, honesty, and long-term commitment to overcome bumpy times, but for the work we do, this kind of dialogue is key."

Today, Roca is at the forefront of innovation to reduce recidivism, largely as a result of Molly and her team's ability to work with gangs, police, courts, parole boards, schools, and social service agencies as effective collaborators. They are becoming an exemplar for work that marries youth justice and strong, safe communities, contributing to a wider shift in developing effective interventions for young adults in the justice system.

We have only just begun to discover the pathways forward

From this place—a new way of being, liberated from our attachment to the bait—what becomes visible as a course of action? What are the pathways for you as an individual and as a part of a collective that may allow you to fulfill your aspirations?

We are certain that we don't know the answers to those questions. If we've done our job well, we've equipped you to generate conversations full of healthy creative tension, inside of which you can't possibly know what will emerge. We wrote this book so that our readers would generate pathways, walk along them, produce stunning results, and share them with us.

What we have envisioned and observed so far is the following sampling of possible alternative pathways. These are new approaches to try when you face the specific pitfalls we identified in chapter 4 (table 3). However, we will leave it to you to identify the pitfalls and possible pathways within your own movement.

Table 6 Pathways forward

Pitfall	Possible alternative pathways
Someone should	• Make our own authentic commitments, and follow through.
Holier than thou	• Invite others to express what future they want for themselves and their grandchildren, and actually listen. • Authentically share our own process and struggles of learning and development. • Identify shared values or commitments, the places where we honor one another's values.
I know what progress is	• Acknowledge people's commitments and honor their contribution. • Invite a vibrant ecology of creative and transformative activity, defined by mutual respect, mutual inspiration, and cocreation.
Lone wolf	• Acknowledge others' commitments. • Share our personal commitments. • Invite others to participate. • Acknowledge our interdependence with others.
It's the right thing to do.	• Listen to what others value and find ways to accomplish multiple goals. • Explore the business/self-interest case and the pro-social case together. Acknowledge that people usually care about both but believe there must be a trade-off.
Selfless OR selfish	• Acknowledge when trade-offs have occurred between the good of the few and the good of the whole. • Honor both as valid and pursue ways to "do well by doing good." • Pursue alignment of personal, societal, and planetary flourishing.
Right now!	• Find synergistic opportunities for K–12 education in any endeavor. • Take time to engage people who have not been part of the movement but who may bring valuable perspectives. • Create opportunities for conversation about our common future, not just the immediate challenge.

Continued on next page

Table 6 (*continued*)

Pitfall	Possible alternative pathways
Humans OR nature	• Acknowledge when trade-offs have occurred between human and other species' well-being. • Honor and express our love for humans and all life. • Get creative about solutions that contribute toward both.
Problem orientation	• Get clear on what you really want to have happen—vision and aspiration. • Take a clear, data-rich view of current reality and redescribe problems as a gap between that current reality and the vision, without jumping to diagnosis or solution. • Organize conversations that are future based, building from a vision of where we want to be and working backward to the present to plot a course toward how we can get there.

Exercise 30
Create pathways for yourself and your movement

Consider the pathways for action in table 6. Which of these pathways might be most valuable for you and your group, organization, or movement? For example:

• Which pitfall best captures the moments where you have collectively gotten stuck? You may wish to review the details of these sample pitfalls in chapter 4.

• Which pathways could best carry you out of that pitfall and help you avoid it in the future?

• Which pathway seems most counterintuitive to you, most contradictory to your current way of doing things? Consider that as a signal that it might be worth exploring if you are stuck.

What other pitfalls have you identified within your movement? Remember, a pitfall is a conversation or group of conversations that correlate with the experience of being stuck.

What other possible pathways might you envision?

Consider the particular individuals, groups, or organizations that you would most like to engage with to advance your goals. Which of the pathways may shift the conversation with them?

What is your next step?

Engage in this inquiry with others within your family and in classrooms, organizations, and communities. Invite others to a conversation about the future they want to create—for themselves, for their grandchildren, and for people they've never met. Just as we have dug collective pitfalls for ourselves, we can create collective pathways forward. You can create a possibility; we can create new possibilities together.

In this process, we can be humble and patient because sometimes the first outcomes are "just" conversations. And we can be bold, taking on the conversations that matter most.

Exercise 31
Commit to action

Consider that powerfully engaging with five particular people in the world would make an extraordinary difference in the realization of your goals for yourself and the world. Who are these people?

You might not know their names. You may just know their organizations and roles.

Do your best to write down that list.

You may have no idea how to access those people. In that case, add people to the top of the list who would be your access to the people you ultimately want to engage.

You may have no idea how to start the conversation. In that case, add people to the top of the list who would be your confidants or peer coaches to help you take steps forward.

Consider that your group or organization may have a reputation because of its pitfalls, such that you have to work through issues internally before you can take pathways forward as a group. In that case, add people to the top of the list whom you would have to engage in your own organization.

Using the tools of this book, do the necessary reflection and planning for the conversations on your list. If baggage needs to be released, use the tools of chapter 6 to bring the conversation back to life. If you are ready to move forward but anticipate a tension you have to navigate, use the chapter 7 tools to embrace the tension.

Out of this landscape of conversations, choose at least one that you can commit to having. Write down in your calendar or journal your commitment to action and the specific deadline by which you will do it.

Imagine if we did this work. Imagine that movements toward a better world are inviting inquiries characterized by bold conversations and healthy spaces of possibility.

A whole new discourse is possible in conversations toward economic, social, and environmental change. We can transform tensions from sources of stuckness and polarization into drivers of creativity and innovation. Rather than being a source of frustration, our movements can become a source of flourishing on the way toward the flourishing of all life. As that happens, our efforts will be inviting and expansive. They will hold more and more diverse people and viewpoints. They will grow to the quality and scale needed to create a world that works for all. Along the way, we will improve our relationships with the people who matter most in our lives and we will more fully and authentically express ourselves.

May you take on significant challenges to humanity and find within them profound opportunities to express our humanity.

Let's get to work.

chapter 8 summary

- As you practice the skills you have learned in this book, you will gain the courage and ability to break through gridlock and polarization on a wider and wider stage. We can never know where our conversations will lead.

- With some shared reflection in our organizations and movements, we can also enhance our collective efficacy. Rather than being a site of frustration and burnout, our movements can become a source of flourishing for the people involved—on the way toward the flourishing of society and the environment.

- Movements get internally polarized around core tensions specific to their goals, as well as a pervasive tension between realist/incrementalist and visionary approaches. Identifying these core tensions can be an essential step in being more unified and effective.

- Movements fall into collective pitfalls that are analogous to those at the individual level. Moving forward means collectively letting go of right, righteous, certain, and safe. In doing so, we can inquire into new ways of seeing the world, new strategies, and the deeper vision and possibility of our work.

- *Pathways* are new ways of being and new strategies for engagement that open up avenues through gridlock and polarization. We offer some examples, but we look to our readers to help chart the course.

- *Do the work*: With others in your organization and movement, inquire into the core tensions of your movement and the places where you have fallen into collective pitfalls. Clarify your vision and the deeper possibilities of your work together. Identify and try out new pathways for action where you have previously gotten stuck. Make personal commitments to have bold conversations and follow through.

Notes

Chapter 1

1. We originally heard this story from Marshall Ganz at the Harvard Kennedy School, who was part of Cesar Chavez's extended team and later applied the lessons when training organizers for Barack Obama's first presidential campaign. This version of the story comes from Jeffrey David Stauch, *Effective Frontline Fundraising: A Guide for Nonprofits, Political Candidates, and Advocacy Groups* (Berkeley, CA: Apress, 2011).

2. Paul Hawken. *The Ecology of Commerce: A Declaration of Sustainability* (New York: Harper Business, 1993).

3. You can read more about Ray Anderson in his books *Mid-Course Correction: Toward a Sustainable Enterprise: The Interface Model* (Atlanta: Peregrinzilla Press, 1998); and *Confessions of a Radical Industrialist: Profits, People, Purpose—Doing Business by Respecting the Earth*, with Robin White (New York: St. Martin's Press, 2009).

4. The algorithms that search engines and social networks use to filter content for "relevance" can contribute to this phenomenon by showing us only news and views that confirm our beliefs. See Eli Pariser's book *The Filter Bubble: What the Internet Is Hiding from You* (New York: Penguin Press, 2011).

5. The classics include Machiavelli's *The Prince* and Sun Tzu's *The Art of War*. But many authors have applied their lessons in contemporary contexts, bolstered by contemporary research on the psychology of power and influence. See Jeffrey Pfeffer, *Power: Why Some People Have It and Others Don't* (New York: Collins Business, 2010); and

Robert B. Cialdini, *Influence: The Psychology of Persuasion* (New York: Collins, 2007).

6. See the idea of "Best Alternative to Negotiated Agreement," or BATNA, in Roger Fisher, William Ury, and Bruce Patton, *Getting to Yes: Negotiating Agreement without Giving In* (New York: Penguin Books, 1991).

7. Daniel C. Esty and Andrew S. Winston. *Green to Gold: How Smart Companies Use Environmental Strategy to Innovate, Create Value, and Build Competitive Advantage* (New Haven, CT: Yale University Press, 2006).

8. George Lakoff, *The All New Don't Think of an Elephant! Know Your Values and Frame the Debate* (White River Junction, VT: Chelsea Green Publishing, 2014).

Chapter 2

1. *Oxford Dictionaries*, s.v. "authentic," accessed April 10, 2016, https://en.oxforddictionaries.com/definition /authentic.

2. We love our dogs. Just for fun, as a student at Yale's Center for Industrial Ecology, Gabriel calculated a rough footprint of the food eaten by his dog Delft using SimaPro, a life-cycle analysis software tool. The environmental cost of Delft's dog food was equivalent to swapping out his hybrid Civic for a Hummer. Now, several years later, both Jason and Gabriel have two children each and their dogs. Two kids plus a large dog often has us driving an SUV or a van instead of a sedan, which effectively doubles our dogs' footprints. As young environmentalists, we thought dogs were good, SUVs were bad. Turns out the world is more complicated than that.

3. Our model of static and dynamic authenticity is inspired by existential philosophy. For a pragmatic exploration of this idea, see Viktor Frankl's *Man's Search for Meaning*, in which he shares the idea that "everything can be

taken from a man but one thing: the last of the human freedoms—to choose one's attitude in any given set of circumstances, to choose one's own way." Victor E. Frankl, *Man's Search for Meaning* (Boston: Beacon Press, 2006).

For a summary of existential philosophy on authenticity and being, see Steven Crowell, "Existentialism," *Stanford University Encyclopedia of Philosophy*, August 23, 2004, http://plato.stanford.edu/entries/existentialism/#Aut.

4. *Oxford Dictionaries*, s.v. "authentic."
5. See Werner H. Ehrhard, Michael C. Jensen, and Kari L. Granger, "Creating Leaders: An Ontological/Phenomenological Model," chap. 16 in *The Handbook for Teaching Leadership: Knowing, Doing, and Being*, eds. Scott A. Snook, Nitin Nohria, and Rakesh Khurana (Thousand Oaks, CA: SAGE Publications, 2012). Abstract available at SSRN, https://ssrn.com/abstract=1881682.

Chapter 3

1. A *being* or *ontological* inquiry in pursuit of a better world is far from a new idea. Psychoanalyst Erich Fromm identified our Western focus on *having* rather than *being* as a core challenge to the flourishing of individuals and the sustainability of humanity. Scholars John Ehrenfeld and Isabel Rimanoczy have more recently emphasized a prioritization of being before doing as a core shift in mindset that allows leaders to craft a better world.
2. See Robert Kegan and Lisa Lahey's work, particularly *Immunity to Change*, which offers further tools and a process for reflection and personal development. Robert Kegan and Lisa Laskow Lahey, "Uncovering the Immunity to Change," chap. 2 in *Immunity to Change: How to Overcome It and Unlock the Potential in Yourself and Your Organization* (Boston: Harvard Business Press, 2009).

3. The word cloud was created from the responses of workshop participants. The size of the word represents the frequency of its occurrence in participant responses.

4. Adapted from Nadia Y. Bashir et al., "The Ironic Impact of Activists: Negative Stereotypes Reduce Social Change Influence," *European Journal of Social Psychology* 43, no. 7 (2013): 614–626, doi:10.1002/ejsp.1983.

Chapter 4

1. Saul D. Alinsky, *Rules for Radicals: A Practical Primer for Realistic Radicals* (New York: Vintage Books, 1989).

2. The pitfall model is inspired by several self-reflective communication models that help people identify their bait, payoff, or secondary gain. The first is developmental psychologists Kegan and Lahey's model of "visible commitments" and "competing commitments." This model is available in their books *How the Way We Talk Can Change the Way We Work* and *Immunity to Change*.

   The second is the idea that people get under-the-table payoffs for maintaining the status quo, from Steve Zaffron and David Logan, *The Three Laws of Performance: Rewriting the Future of Your Organization and Your Life* (San Francisco: Jossey-Bass, 2009), 58.

   Crucial Conversations also mentions payoffs and is a resource we recommend. We chose to create a new terminology and metaphor to focus attention on the collective aspect of pitfalls—they are common among advocates for a better world, often shared by members of a community or movement. Kerry Patterson et al., *Crucial Conversations: Tools for Talking When the Stakes Are High* (New York: McGraw-Hill, 2012).

3. Idries Shah, "How to Catch Monkeys," in *Tales of the Dervishes: Teaching-Stories of the Sufi Masters over the Past 1000 Years* (London: Octagon Press, 1982), 29.

4. Showing a video of a monkey getting trapped by a hunter is not always a great fit for any audience! Fortunately, the hunter's purpose in this video is to feed the monkey salty foods, release him, and then chase him as he leads the way to a secret source of spring water. "The Monkey Trap Is Not a Lemmings Myth," YouTube, posted by Russell Wright, October 13, 2011, https://www.youtube.com/watch?v=oAyU6wZ_ZUg.

5. See Kegan and Lahey, "Uncovering the Immunity to Change."

6. Chris Argyris, in his study of why people resist feedback and learning in organizations, identified a similar list of motivations: people seek to be in control, to maximize winning, to suppress negative feelings, and to be rational. Chris Argyris, *Teaching Smart People How to Learn* (Boston: Harvard Business Press, 2008).

Chapter 5

1. Instead, consider that everyone is internally motivated and inquire into what internally motivates you and what internally motivates others. For support in this journey, see Susan Fowler's *Why Motivating People Doesn't Work . . . and What Does* (San Francisco: Berrett-Koehler, 2014).

2. For a deeper inquiry into the linkages between positive psychology and creating a better world, see Gabriel B. Grant, "Transforming Sustainability," *Journal of Corporate Citizenship* 2012, no. 46, 123–137, doi:10.9774/gleaf.4700.2012.su.00008.

3. Scharmer, C. Otto, *Theory U: Leading from the Future as It Emerges* (San Francisco: Berrett-Koehler, 2009).

4. Special thanks to Barrett Brown for the meditation in exercise 17. He crafted the first variation for a workshop at the 2014 Flourish and Prosper Conference.

5. The word cloud was created from the responses of workshop participants. The size of the word represents the frequency of its occurrence in participant responses.
6. Scharmer, *Theory U.*

Chapter 6

1. For peer-reviewed research on the elements of good apologies, see Karina Schumann, "An Affirmed Self and a Better Apology: The Effect of Self-Affirmation on Transgressors' Responses to Victims," Journal of Experimental Social Psychology 54 (2014): 89–96, doi: 10.1016 /j.jesp.2014.04.013.

   For a fantastic guidebook on effective apology, see John Kador, *Effective Apology: Mending Fences, Building Bridges, and Restoring Trust* (San Francisco: Berrett-Koehler, 2009).
2. Halfhearted apologies may backfire on you. Take full responsibility if you are committed to moving forward. See Jennifer K. Robbennolt, "Apologies and Legal Settlement: An Empirical Examination," *Michigan Law Review* 102, no. 3 (2003): 460–516, doi:10.2307/3595367.
3. Research documents the psychological payoffs. By not apologizing, you can feel in control and better about yourself in the moment. Tyler G. Okimoto, Michael Wenzel, and Kyli Hedrick, "Refusing to Apologize Can Have Psychological Benefits (and We Issue No Mea Culpa for This Research Finding)," *European Journal of Social Psychology* 43, no. 1 (2012): 22–31, doi:10.1002/ejsp.1901.
4. Gabriel cofounded the Byron Fellowship Educational Foundation to activate emerging leaders, engaging their unique abilities to cultivate generative efforts within their own communities (www.byronfellowship.org).

Chapter 7

1. Dan Kahan at Yale's Cultural Cognition Project has shown how values and ideology can shape people's perception of technological and environmental risks. Conservatives systematically underestimate the risk of climate change, while liberals systematically overestimate the risk of nuclear power and concealed handguns. Dan M. Kahan, Hank Jenkins-Smith, and Donald Braman, "Cultural Cognition of Scientific Consensus," *SSRN Electronic Journal*, doi:10.2139/ssrn.1549444.

2. Haidt's book *The Righteous Mind* is a fantastic resource, inviting readers to explore the emotional, cultural, and evolutionary foundations of our morality and politics, building on decades of research into cultural and political psychology. Jonathan Haidt, *The Righteous Mind: Why Good People Are Divided by Politics and Religion* (New York: Pantheon Books, 2012).

3. "Carl the Cuck Slayer vs Van Jones," Van Jones interview by Owen Shroyer, YouTube, posted by TheInfowarrior, July 21, 2016, https://www.youtube.com/watch?v=sjtENUXgZIY.

4. We've changed the specifics of the graphs to simplify them and make them more general than the investment management context.

Chapter 8

1. Tom Kludt, "Mike Pence Appears at Odds with Trump on Climate Change," CNN, September 27, 2016, http://www.cnn.com/2016/09/27/politics/mike-pence-donald-trump-climate-change-trade/.

2. For more exploration of the idea of creative tension, see Peter Senge's book *The Fifth Discipline* and the fieldbooks that follow it. Peter M. Senge, *The Fifth Discipline: The*

Art and Practice of the Learning Organization (New York: Doubleday/Currency, 1990). Also see Robert Fritz's work that was Senge and his team's original inspiration. Robert Fritz, *The Path of Least Resistance: Learning to Become the Creative Force in Your Own Life* (New York: Ballantine, 1989).

3. John Tillman Lyle, *Regenerative Design for Sustainable Development* (New York: John Wiley, 1994); John R. Ehrenfeld and Andrew J. Hoffman, *Flourishing: A Frank Conversation about Sustainability* (Stanford, CA: Stanford Business Books, 2013); and Yossi Sheffi, *The Power of Resilience: How the Best Companies Manage the Unexpected* (Cambridge, MA: MIT Press, 2015).

4. The word cloud was created from the responses of workshop participants. The size of the word represents the frequency of its occurrence in participant responses.

5. Rumi, *The Essential Rumi*, trans. Coleman Barks (San Francisco: Harper, 1995).

6. John R. Ehrenfeld, *Flourishing by Design*, http://www .johnehrenfeld.com/.

7. Quoted in Peter Senge, Hal Hamilton, and John Kania, "The Dawn of System Leadership," *Stanford Social Innovation Review*, Winter 2015, https://ssir.org/articles /entry/the_dawn_of_system_leadership.

Bibliography

Alinsky, Saul. *Rules for Radicals: A Practical Primer for Realistic Radicals.* New York: Vintage Books, 1989.

Anderson, Ray C. *Confessions of a Radical Industrialist: Profits, People, Purpose—Doing Business by Respecting the Earth.* With Robin A. White. New York: St. Martin's Press, 2009.

———— *Mid-Course Correction: Toward a Sustainable Enterprise: The Interface Model.* Atlanta: Peregrinzilla Press, 1998.

Argyris, Chris. *Teaching Smart People How to Learn.* Boston: Harvard Business Press, 2008.

Bashir, Nadia Y., Penelope Lockwood, Alison L. Chasteen, Daniel Nadolny, and Indra Noyes. "The Ironic Impact of Activists: Negative Stereotypes Reduce Social Change Influence." *European Journal of Social Psychology* 43, no. 7 (2013): 614–626. doi:10.1002/ejsp.1983.

"Carl the Cuck Slayer vs Van Jones." Van Jones interview by Owen Shroyer. YouTube. Posted by TheInfowarrior. July 21, 2016. https://www.youtube.com/watch?v=sjtENUXgZIY.

Cialdini, Robert B. *Influence: The Psychology of Persuasion.* New York: Collins, 2007.

Crowell, Steven. "Existentialism." *Stanford University Encyclopedia of Philosophy.* August 23, 2004. Accessed November 13, 2016. http://plato.stanford.edu/entries/existentialism/#Aut.

Ehrenfeld, John, R., and Andrew J. Hoffman. *Flourishing: A Frank Conversation about Sustainability.* Stanford, CA: Stanford Business Books, 2013.

Ehrhard, Werner H., Michael C. Jensen, and Kari L. Granger. "Creating Leaders: An Ontological/Phenomenological Model." Chap. 16 in *The Handbook for Teaching Leadership: Knowing, Doing, and Being*, edited by Scott A. Snook, Nitin Nohria, and Rakesh Khurana. Thousand Oaks, CA: SAGE Publications, 2012. Abstract available at SSRN, https://ssrn.com/abstract=1881682.

Ehrenfeld, John R. *Flourishing by Design*. Accessed November 13, 2016. http://www.johnehrenfeld.com/.

Esty, Daniel C., and Andrew S. Winston, *Green to Gold: How Smart Companies Use Environmental Strategy to Innovate, Create Value, and Build Competitive Advantage*. New Haven, CT: Yale University Press, 2006.

Fisher, Roger, William Ury, and Bruce Patton. *Getting to Yes: Negotiating Agreement without Giving In*. New York: Penguin Books, 1991.

Fowler, Susan. *Why Motivating People Doesn't Work . . . and What Does*. San Francisco: Berrett-Koehler, 2014.

Frankl, Viktor E. *Man's Search for Meaning*. Boston: Beacon Press, 2006.

Fritz, Robert. *The Path of Least Resistance: Learning to Become the Creative Force in Your Own Life*. New York: Ballantine, 1989.

Grant, Gabriel B. "Transforming Sustainability." *Journal of Corporate Citizenship* 2012, no. 46, 123–137. doi:10.9774/gleaf.4700.2012.su.00008.

Haidt, Jonathan. *The Righteous Mind: Why Good People Are Divided by Politics and Religion*. New York: Pantheon Books, 2012.

Hawken, Paul. *The Ecology of Commerce: A Declaration of Sustainability*. New York: Harper Business, 1993.

Kador, John. *Effective Apology: Mending Fences, Building Bridges, and Restoring Trust.* San Francisco: Berrett-Koehler, 2009.

Kahan, Dan M., Hank Jenkins-Smith, and Donald Braman. "Cultural Cognition of Scientific Consensus." *SSRN Electronic Journal.* doi:10.2139/ssrn.1549444.

Kegan, Robert, and Lisa Laskow Lahey. *How the Way We Talk Can Change the Way We Work: Seven Languages for Transformation.* San Francisco: Jossey-Bass, 2001.

———. "Uncovering the Immunity to Change." Chap. 2 in *Immunity to Change: How to Overcome It and Unlock Potential in Yourself and Your Organization.* Boston: Harvard Business Press, 2009.

Kludt, Tom. "Mike Pence Appears at Odds with Trump on Climate Change." CNN. September 27, 2016. http://www.cnn.com/2016/09/27/politics/mike-pence-donald-trump-climate-change-trade/.

Lakoff, George. *The All New Don't Think of an Elephant! Know Your Values and Frame the Debate.* White River Junction, VT: Chelsea Green Publishing, 2014.

Lyle, John Tillman. *Regenerative Design for Sustainable Development.* New York: John Wiley, 1994.

Machiavelli, Niccolò. *The Prince.* Translated by W. K. Marriott. Chicago: Encyclopedia Britannica, 1955.

"The Monkey Trap Is Not a Lemmings Myth." YouTube posted by Russell Wright. October 13, 2011. https://www.youtube.com/watch?v=oAyU6wZ_ZUg.

Okimoto, Tyler G., Michael Wenzel, and Kyli Hedrick. "Refusing to Apologize Can Have Psychological Benefits (and We Issue No Mea Culpa for This Research Finding)." *European Journal of Social Psychology* 43, no. 1 (2012): 22–31. doi:10.1002/ejsp.1901.

Oxford Dictionaries. s.v. "authentic." Accessed April 10, 2016. https://en.oxforddictionaries.com/definition/authentic.

Pariser, Eli. *The Filter Bubble: What the Internet Is Hiding from You.* New York: Penguin Press, 2011.

Patterson, Kerry, Joseph Grenny, Ron McMillan, and Al Switzler. *Crucial Conversations: Tools for Talking When the Stakes Are High.* New York: McGraw-Hill, 2012.

Pfeffer, Jeffrey. *Power: Why Some People Have It and Others Don't.* New York: Collins Business, 2010.

Robbennolt, Jennifer K. "Apologies and Legal Settlement: An Empirical Examination." *Michigan Law Review* 102, no. 3 (2003): 460–516. doi:10.2307/3595367.

Rumi. *The Essential Rumi.* Translated by Coleman Barks. San Francisco: Harper, 1995.

Scharmer, C. Otto. *Theory U: Leading from the Future as It Emerges.* San Francisco: Berrett-Koehler, 2009.

Schumann, Karina. "An Affirmed Self and a Better Apology: The Effect of Self-Affirmation on Transgressors' Responses to Victims." *Journal of Experimental Social Psychology* 54 (2014): 89–96. doi:10.1016/j.jesp.2014.04.013.

Senge, Peter M. *The Fifth Discipline: The Art and Practice of the Learning Organization.* New York: Doubleday/Currency, 1990.

Senge, Peter, Hal Hamilton, and John Kania. "The Dawn of System Leadership." *Stanford Social Innovation Review*, Winter 2015. https://ssir.org/articles/entry/the_dawn_of_system_leadership.

Shah, Idries. "How to Catch Monkeys." In *Tales of the Dervishes: Teaching-Stories of the Sufi Masters over the Past 1000 Years*, 29–30. London: Octagon Press, 1982.

Sheffi, Yossi. *The Power of Resilience: How the Best Companies Manage the Unexpected.* Cambridge, MA: MIT Press, 2015.

Stauch, Jeffrey David. *Effective Frontline Fundraising: A Guide for Nonprofits, Political Candidates, and Advocacy Groups.* Berkeley, CA: Apress, 2011.

Sun Tzu. *The Art of War.* Translated by Samuel B. Griffith. London: Oxford University Press, 1971.

Zaffron, Steve, and David Logan. *The Three Laws of Performance: Rewriting the Future of Your Organization and Your Life.* San Francisco: Jossey-Bass, 2009.

Acknowledgments

While most acknowledgment sections end with the authors' families, we think it's most appropriate to start there. Our wives, Alaka and Sarah, and our children, Vikram, Uma, Ari, and Madeleine, have had to put up with more of our nonsense than anyone. And no one has held up as crystal clear a mirror to help us reflect, learn, and grow. In these pages we include some choice excerpts of our crusades on the home front. Sarah provided valuable input on several drafts of the book. Alaka contributed the elegant turns of phrase that reshaped not only the chapter and book titles but our voice throughout. There are no words to express our gratitude for their love, humor, and support through this whole journey.

We have also benefited from a variety of mentors and teachers along the way. For Jason, the key "voices in my head" through writing this book have been (in chronological order) my parents, Rick Jay and Sue Sawyer (who also provided valuable comments on the book), Reb Zalman Schachter-Shalomi, Netanel Miles-Yepez, Robert Kegan, Catalina Laserna, Bruce Allyn, Bill Isaacs, Skip Griffin, Glennifer Gillespie, Peter Senge, John Sterman, Wanda Orlikowski, Rick Locke, and Susan Silbey. For Gabriel, my parents, Gregory Grant and Marilyn Bauchat, who taught me to always pursue my purpose, Jim Brainard, Mark Boyce, Gunter Pauli, Amelia Terrapin, Tom Seager, Marian Chertow, Charles

Vogl, Amy Wrzesniewski, Chad Oliver, Harry Pickens, Anamaria Aristizabal, Wayne Davis, and Barrett Brown.

We both owe a debt of gratitude to a few shared mentors and influencers whose work has inspired ours. John Ehrenfeld redefined sustainability as the possibility that human and other life will flourish on Earth forever. Donella Meadows invited us all to hold and express our vision. Together they helped us identify the critical link between authenticity, personal transformation, and wider social transformation. Robert Kegan and Lisa Lahey's books, including *Immunity to Change*, and Otto Scharmer's *Theory U* have been powerful influences on our work and showed us that sharing a process of personal and social transformation through a book is possible. We also both feel profound gratitude for the chance to encounter Werner Erhard and our teachers and coaches in the lineage he inspired, including some whom we've already mentioned and Roger Smith. They shared with us the possibility of transforming a discourse. In addition, the notion of paradox underlies many of our ideas, particularly in the "Embrace the tension" chapter, and we are thankful to a lineage of work on paradox from Kenwyn Smith and David Berg, Robert Quinn and Kim Cameron, Wendy Smith and Marianne Lewis, and Paula Jarzabkowski. We benefit from their consistent effort to make an esoteric concept useful in understanding organizational and social change. Finally, our work benefits from a set of contemporary authors taking on the challenge of political polarization from new vantage points. Dan Kahan's cultural psychology of climate change and other societal risks, Jonathan Haidt's careful depiction of the "Righteous Mind," and Mark Gerzon's well-documented efforts toward a "Reunited States of America" have all been inspirations for this book.

Our workshop participants, students, and interviewees brought their experience to the table through profoundly vulnerable and powerful stories. They have done the real work of changing the conversation, and we owe all of them our gratitude. A few chose to share their stories in the book and leave what we hope will be an important legacy: Kevin Hagen, Melissa Gildersleeve, Joyce LaValle, John Frey, Sean Kenney, Rob Wilson, Molly Baldwin, and Brent Segal.

None of this would be possible without the cofacilitators we have engaged along the way, including Katie Wallace, Barrett Brown, and Sara Soderstrom. Barrett helped us develop key exercises. Sara's environmental leadership class at the University of Michigan has generated some of the most profound transformations we have witnessed. Our workshops have also enjoyed some financial sponsorship, and we owe particular thanks to Jeff Senne at PwC, Mark Boyce at Byron Fellowship, and Jeremy Grantham and Ramsay Ravenel at the Grantham Foundation for the Protection of the Environment.

We have received tremendous help and inspiration from Laura Yates, our project manager. A glimpse into her spring-break climate change conversation kicks off the book, and stories of her courageous conversations are included in chapters 6 and 8. She kept us organized and on task throughout the whole journey.

Our editors, Rose-Anne Moore and Anna Leinberger, helped wrangle our cacophony of ideas and exercises into a coherent whole. And we would never have pro-ceeded with the book if it weren't for the "tough love" and encouragement of Jeevan Sivasubramaniam and Steve Piersanti at Berrett-Koehler. We are inspired to be part of a publisher and author community that is dedi-cated to creating a world that works for all and that puts its authors through their paces to get there.

We received extremely helpful feedback on our early draft from two groups. The first includes pub-lished authors we respect, like Wanda Orlikowski, Peter Senge, John Ehrenfeld, Andrew Hoffman, Barrett Brown, Charles Vogl, Bill Isaacs, Kate Isaacs, and Steve Schein. Others were "test users" who muddled through our first-draft exercises, including Rachel Payne, Becky Margiotta, Carolyn DuPont, Heather Johnson, Tamara Staton, Bethany Patten, John Harrison, Jasmine Hamilton, and Savannah Christiansen. Sarah Townsend-Grant and Chloe Cockburn helped us bring in perspectives from health and social justice contexts. Our illustrator, John Cox, helped us bring the spirit of serious play alive. And finally, we have greatly benefited from other university faculty who field-tested the work in their classrooms, including Elizabeth Walsh, Jessica Vogt, James Beresford, Jim Stoner, and Glen Dowell.

We have done our best to honor all our friends' exten-sive insights; any further omission or lack of clarity falls squarely on our shoulders.

Index

accountability, 38, 119, 124
action(s), 16, 123–124
  for change, 168–169
  commitment to, 182
  formulas for, 10, 28
activism, scale of, 13
advocacy, 83, 108
agreement, creating, 10
Alinksy, Saul, *Rules for Radicals*,
  62
ambivalence, 138, 140, 151
Anderson, Ray, 12
apologies/apologizing
  coming clean, 117
  effects of, 113, 127
  elements of effective, 114,
    115–116
  example, 117–121
  vulnerability in, 120
aspirations. *See* future/future
  aspirations
assumptions, 38, 60, 142, 170
authenticity
  in conversations, 29
  definitions/descriptions, 30
  dynamic (*see* dynamic
    authenticity)
  static, 33, 39
  your notions of, 34–35
  See also inauthenticity

background conversations
  bait in the trap in, 78, 79
  identifying your, 79
  patterns in, 67

pitfalls in, 68–73
transforming, 51–53
ways of being in, 64
baggage of conversations, 41–43,
  60, 127. *See also* conversations;
  ways of being
bait/bait in the trap
  acknowledging our, 127
  examples, 61–62, 68–73
  forms of bait, 75, 76–78, 81
  "How to Catch Monkeys"
    story, 74
  identifying the, 74, 78, 79, 175
  letting go of the, 80, 108, 164,
    170
  locating the collective, 169–
    170
  as metaphor, 62, 64–65
  your relationship to, 162–163
  See also pitfalls
Baldwin, Molly, 176–177
barriers to conversations, 125
Bashir, Nadia, 49–50
becoming, 45
being certain, 76, 167–168, 170
being/getting stuck
  apologizing and, 116
  approaches to issues of,
    28
  collateral damage as cost of,
    66
  consistency with the past and,
    30–31
  in conversations, 16, 18–20,
    47–48

About the Authors

Jason Jay

Jason grew up in Boulder, Colorado, where he lived in awe of snowy mountains and watched his parents build a business that improved people's lives. He moved to Boston and fell in love with his wife, Alaka, and life in a coastal city. Alaka's family in India made him their own and helped him see the world as fundamentally interconnected. He grew to understand how all these places he loves are fragile and committed himself to seeing them flourish for his children, Vikram and Uma, to enjoy with their children.

Today, Jason is a senior lecturer and the director of the Sustainability Initiative at the MIT Sloan School of Management. He teaches courses on strategy and innovation for sustainable business to hundreds of leaders every year. Through his writing, teaching, and community building, he empowers business leaders to help their organizations thrive while tackling the tough social and environmental challenges of our time. Before he began teaching, he ran an Internet start-up, traveled around the world, taught kindergarten, received a bachelor's degree in psychology and a master's in education from Harvard University, worked as a consultant with Dialogos International, and earned a doctorate in organization studies from MIT.

Gabriel Grant

When Gabriel was a child, his parents went to work each day to contribute toward making the world a better place. He couldn't wait to grow up and do the same. Over the past fifteen years, he has trained more than one thousand purpose-driven leaders and world-class change agents, including sustainability directors and vice presidents from more than 150 major brands. He came to see that when people experience their work as a calling, they come alive and contribute to the flourishing of all life around them. He envisions a world where people share their whole selves, just as they are, just as they're not, and as who they want to become.

Today Gabriel's work supports organizations in creating cultures of purpose, trust, and engagement. He is the CEO of Human Partners and cofounder of the Byron Fellowship Educational Foundation. He holds a bachelor's degree in physics and a master's in ecological systems engineering from Purdue University and a master's in leadership and sustainability from Yale University. His research at Yale explored the relationships between micro-level flourishing of individuals, flourishing organizations and communities, and a flourishing planet. He lives in Seattle with his wife, Sarah, and daughters, Ariana and Madeleine with whom he shares a mission of creating unconditional love and powerfully contributing to others.

Berrett–Koehler
Publishers

Connecting people and ideas
to create a world that works for all

Dear Reader,

Thank you for picking up this book and joining our worldwide community of Berrett-Koehler readers. We share ideas that bring positive change into people's lives, organizations, and society.

To welcome you, we'd like to offer you a free e-book. You can pick from among twelve of our bestselling books by entering the promotional code **BKP92E** here: http://www.bkconnection.com/welcome.

When you claim your free e-book, we'll also send you a copy of our e-newsletter, the *BK Communiqué*. Although you're free to unsubscribe, there are many benefits to sticking around. In every issue of our newsletter you'll find

- A free e-book
- Tips from famous authors
- Discounts on spotlight titles
- Hilarious insider publishing news
- A chance to win a prize for answering a riddle

Best of all, our readers tell us, "Your newsletter is the only one I actually read." So claim your gift today, and please stay in touch!

Sincerely,

Charlotte Ashlock
Steward of the BK Website

Questions? Comments? Contact me at bkcommunity@bkpub.com.